The Best of
SWEDISH
COOKING
& BAKING

The Best of
SWEDISH
COOKING
& BAKING

By Marianne Grönwall van der Tuuk

Traditional and Modern
Swedish Dishes

From SWEDISH COOKING AT ITS BEST and SWEDISH
BAKING AT ITS BEST, published by Wezäta Forlag,
Göteborg, Sweden.

RAND MⸯNALLY & COMPANY
CHICAGO / NEW YORK / SAN FRANCISCO

Contents

Hints for using this book

Every effort has been made to make the recipes in this book as clear and detailed as possible, so that even a beginner should be able to follow them with ease.

The name of each dish is given in English and Swedish.

When capital letters are used in the text, as in "serve with Mashed Potatoes", a recipe for the capitalized dish is given in the book.

All recipes which contain flour, have been tested with American all-purpose flour. If this book is used in Sweden or other European countries, flour quantities may have to be increased depending on the quality. For the exact weight, see table below.

In the section on Baking, every recipe specifies what particular kind of fat to use, and only by following this specification will the best result be obtained.

CONVERTING TABLE
for weights and measurements

The ingredients in the recipes in this book are given in American standard measurements. All measurements are level. For other measurements use this table of equivalents.

1 cup liquid = $^1/_2$ pint (scant) = $2^1/_4$ decilitres
1 cup butter = $^1/_2$ pound = 225 grams
1 cup sifted all-purpose flour = 4 ounces = $2^1/_4$ decilitres = 125 grams
1 cup cake flour = 1 cup all-purpose flour less 2 tablespoons
$^1/_2$ cup egg whites = 3 large or 4 small egg whites
1 cup sugar = 7 ounces = $2^1/_4$ decilitres = .190 grams
1 cake compressed yeast = 1 ounce = 30 grams
1 tablespoon unflavored gelatin = about 4–5 Swedish leaves of gelatin
  (Thickens 2 cups of liquid)

The American measuring cup is 8 fl. oz. If the British cup of half-pint size, recently made a standard for kitchen measuring cups, is used, the results will be proportionately larger.

Finally, some good advice, read each recipe all through before you start so that you know how to proceed.

Introduction

THIS BOOK COMPRISES a selection of the most popular traditional Swedish dishes and many new ones as well which more recently have been incorporated with the Swedish cuisine. They are chosen with an eye to their suitability and attractiveness for modern taste. From my own experience as an American homemaker, I have tried to select the Swedish dishes which especially appeal to the American taste and which, I think, may become favorites in American homes.

Each recipe has been carefully tested and will give perfect results if you follow the directions exactly. The many illustrations both in black and white and in color will, I hope, inspire you to make the food you prepare look attractive and artistic, in the best Swedish tradition.

The recipes in the section on Swedish Baking were chosen from the best liked and most well-known Swedish baking recipes. Some are very old and have been handed down through generations in my own family.

This selection represents the result of ten years of effort in converting Swedish recipes to usable American ones. I found that the difference between Swedish and American flour, spices, etc., made it necessary to establish what quantities to substitute, so that the same delicate flavors would result, as with my original baking recipes in Sweden. For many years I worked as a home economist in the U.S.A., and this proved to be of invaluable help finally to overcome all obstacles and to incorporate time-saving methods, using American appliances.

The interest in good, homebaked cakes, pastries and cookies is very great in Sweden. Swedish people like to have something sweet with their coffee, which they seldom drink alone. Therefore, you will find many delicacies created for different occasions: the fragrant Saffron Buns for the Lucia celebration, the crisp, spicy Ginger Snaps for Christmas, just to mention a few. You will also find in the Cookie chapter the really delicate Brandy Ring, which is one of the old-fashioned, time-consuming, but worthwhile recipes which I have included along with many good "quickies" which are the kind of cookies mostly found in Sweden today.

Most of the dishes and accessories that you see in the pictures are typical old or modern Swedish products which can be found in a number of gift stores or in well-stocked department stores throughout America. I am indebted to the following porcelain manufacturing companies: AB Rörstrands Porslinsfabriker, AB Gustavsbergs Fabriker, and Upsala Ekeby AB, as well as to the Handicraft Association of Göteberg for lending me many of their articles for the pictures.

My appreciation and thanks go to all who gave me friendly help with this book—to Märta Holmgren, who is in charge of my Swedish publisher's own test kitchen; to Al Reagan, art director of the *Farm Journal,* for his valuable advice in planning the color pictures; to Sixten Sandell for his tireless cooperation in taking the color photographs; and to my husband, Anthony van der Tuuk, for his many good suggestions.

I hope that THE BEST OF SWEDISH COOKING & BAKING will find its way into many homes in the English-speaking world where a change from everyday food is appreciated, and that it may add a different flavor and appearance to many a party buffet.

Mamaroneck, N. Y. November, 1965

Marianne Grönwall van der Tuuk

6

The Best of
SWEDISH
COOKING

The Smörgåsbord

Swedish cooking has become famous through the Smörgåsbord. Although there is much more than this to Swedish cooking, just mentioning a Smörgåsbord brings to mind an abundance of delicate dishes. You will find the Smörgåsbord in small and large restaurants in many parts of the world and its popularity is still steadily increasing. It is appropriate then that we begin this book by introducing you to the Smörgåsbord, but one which is not too heavy for modern taste, nor too complicated for the modern homemaker.

A traditional Smörgåsbord always starts with bread and butter, and one or more herring dishes, generally accompanied by small boiled potatoes. If you want your Smörgåsbord to be really Swedish, serve several warm and cold herring dishes; but for people who are not familiar with this kind of salty food, one dish is usually enough. (The herring dish I have found most popular in foreign countries is the *Gourmet Herring*.) However, you might add a few small dishes like the *Bird's Nest* and *Anchovies Piquant*.

After the salty food, change the plates and follow with some cold egg dishes, *Eggs with Caviar*, or *Eggs with Mayonnaise and Shrimp* for example. Then serve different kinds of salads, such as the *West Coast Salad*, or *Italian Salad*, with different kinds of cold sliced meat, tongue, ham, roast beef, veal with *Pickled Fresh Cucumber*.

For a more elaborate Smörgåsbord, include some dishes in aspic. *Chicken Aspic* or *Poached Salmon in Aspic* look very elegant and "showy".

The typical Swedish way of rounding out the meal is to serve a variety of small warm dishes, such as *Kidney Sauté, Small Meatballs, Stuffed Onions* and filled omelets. This may be omitted of course if you have served *Potato Salad* with the cold meats. Finish the Smörgåsbord with some good cheese on Swedish rye crisp bread and top it all off with good strong coffee.

You will find here the best of the good, old-fashioned recipes as

9

well as many fine modern ones, all of them adapted to the modern homemaker. Almost every recipe can be prepared ahead of time, which, for entertaining purposes, is the great advantage of the Smörgåsbord. Since the dishes may be served separately as well as together, they can serve many purposes. They solve the problem of before-dinner tidbits and spreads, or provide you with an unusual hors d'œuvres, a light main course or a successful buffet supper.

ANCHOVY EYE

SOLÖGA

8 Swedish anchovy fillets, minced
1 tablespoon minced onion
1 egg yolk

To make the "Eye" place egg yolk in center of a small serving plate; arrange minced onion in ring around egg yolk, the anchovies as an outer ring around onion. See color picture of Smörgåsbord between pp. 14 and 15 The first person to help himself to the dish stirs all ingredients together, blending well.

Or, if you don't want to make the raw "Eye", mix all ingredients together and fry quickly in butter.

Serve on crackers or toast.

Pickled Salt Herring
Inlagd sill

PICKLED SALT HERRING

INLAGD SILL

This is a "must" on a true smörgåsbord.

1 large salt herring

Dressing:
$1/2$ cup vinegar
2 tablespoons water
$1/3$ cup sugar
2 tablespoons chopped onions
5 peppercorns, crushed
10 whole allspice, crushed
2 sprigs fresh dill

Garnish:
fresh dill sprigs
onion rings

Clean herring, removing head. Rinse under cold running water. Soak in cold water 10–12 hours, changing water a few times so the herring will not be too salty. You could start the soaking a few hours before going to bed, changing water a few times, and then leaving to soak over night.

11

Cut herring along backbone. Remove the big backbone and as many small ones as possible; pull off skin. The bones come out easily after the soaking. Drain fillets on absorbent paper, then place fillets together, one on top of the other, so that they look like a whole fish. Cut into thin slices with sharp knife. Slide spatula under sliced fish and remove to a long narrow dish, see picture page 11.

Mix all dressing ingredients together in a saucepan. Bring to the boiling point and simmer for a few minutes. Cool and strain. Pour over herring. Garnish with a few sprigs of fresh dill and some raw onion rings on top, see color picture opposite page 14.

Cover dish with aluminum foil and refrigerate a few hours before serving; or better still, let stand in refrigerator over night – the longer it stands the better the seasonings blend.

Serve with small boiled potatoes on the Smörgåsbord.

HERRING SALAD   SILLSALLAD

1 salt herring or 2 Matjes herring fillets in wine-flavored sauce	¼ cup finely chopped onion
	4 tablespoons vinegar or liquid from pickled beets
1½ cups diced boiled potatoes	2 tablespoons water
1½ cups diced pickled beets	2 tablespoons sugar
⅓ cup diced dill pickles	dash of pepper
½ cup diced apple	2 hard-cooked eggs

If Matjes herring fillets are used, they need no preparation except to be minced finely. If salt herring is used, clean fish, removing head. Soak fish 10-12 hours, changing water a few times so fish will not be too salty. If you wish, start soaking fish 3 or 4 hours before you go to bed, change water a few times, and soak over night. Bone and fillet as in Pickled Salt Herring, see page 11. Dice fillets.

Now, finely mince all the diced ingredients so the flavors will blend as they should. Mix them together thoroughly but carefully – they should not be mashed.

Combine vinegar, water, sugar and pepper; blend well. Gently stir into fish mixture. Pack into a 5-cup mold that has been rinsed with cold water or brushed lightly with salad oil. Chill in refrigerator a few hours.

Unmold onto serving platter and garnish with hard-cooked eggs and chopped parsley, see color picture opposite page 8. Serve with sour cream.

Makes 6–8 servings.

Bird's Nest
Fågelbo

BIRD'S NEST   FÅGELBO

Bird's Nest is a classic dish for a Swedish Smörgåsbord and is good both to look at and to eat.

5 Swedish anchovy fillets, chopped
1 tablespoon chopped onion
1 tablespoon capers
1 tablespoon chopped chives
2 tablespoons diced pickled beets
1 tablespoon diced cold boiled potato
2 raw egg yolks

Arrange each of the ingredients in a separate mound on a small serving plate, placing the mounds so that they form one large or two small nest-like circles. Depress center mounds slightly and carefully place egg yolks in depression to give you a filled bird's nest, see picture above.

The first person to help himself to the dish stirs all the ingredients together until well blended.

If the dish is prepared ahead of time, cover with aluminum foil and keep in refrigerator until serving time.

13

CHEF'S PICKLED HERRING
GLASMÄSTARSILL

This kind of herring you will find almost everywhere in America to-day, so popular has it become.

2 salt herring
1 tablespoon whole allspice,
   crushed
2 bay leaves
1/2 teaspoon mustard seed
1 small piece horseradish, diced,   *Dressing:*
   or 1 teaspoon bottled horseradish   1 cup vinegar
2 onions, sliced   1/4 cup water
1/2 carrot, sliced   1/2 cup sugar

Clean fish, removing heads. Soak fish in cold water 10–12 hours, changing water a few times so fish will not be too salty. If you wish, start soaking a few hours before you go to bed; change water a few times, then soak over night.

Drain fish on absorbent paper. Cut crosswise into 1/2-inch slices without removing bones and place in a glass jar. Arrange herring and remaining ingredients in alternate layers in glass jar.

Combine dressing ingredients and bring to the boiling point. Chill. Pour over herring, cover and let stand a few days in refrigerator before serving. Always serve this kind of herring from the jar.

Taste improves, the longer the herring is pickled.

PART OF A TRADITIONAL SMÖRGÅSBORD

is pictured on the colorspread found between pp. 14 and 15. You will see, on the elevated part, from left to right: Gourmet Herring. Chicken Aspic. A tossed salad. A tray with an assortment of cheese and a dish with butter balls.

Below on the table from left to right: Sliced, smoked salmon. Anchovy Eye. Lobster salad. Radishes. Sliced ham with asparagus. Brown Beans, Swedish Style. Small Meatballs. A round platter with different kinds of cold, sliced meat. Stuffed Eggs and carrot sticks. French Omelet with Creamed Mushrooms. Pickled beets and pickled cucumber. Herring au Gratin. Poached Salmon in Aspic. A tray with different kinds of canned Herring and small boiled potatoes.

CHRISTMAS EVE SUPPER
with Pickled Salt Herring. Herring Salad. Liver Pâté. Pork Sausage. Home-Cured Christmas Ham and Christmas Wine

Preparing Janssons Temptation
Beredning av Janssons frestelse

JANSSONS TEMPTATION (ANCHOVIES AU GRATIN)

JANSSONS FRESTELSE

This dish is a real temptation when served on a Smörgåsbord, or as an appetizer.

1 cup sliced onions (1½ onions)
⅓ cup butter or margarine
4 cups raw potatoes, cut into thin strips

1 can Swedish anchovy fillets (about 18 fillets)
1 cup cream

Sauté sliced onions in 2 tablespoons of the butter or margarine.

Peel potatoes and cut into very thin strips see picture above.

Butter a 1½-quart baking dish. Arrange one layer of half the amount of potatoes, spread onions and anchovy fillets over and top with remaining potatoes. Sprinkle 1 tablespoon juice from anchovy can over potatoes and dot with remaining butter or margarine. Add cream and cover with aluminum foil.

Bake in hot oven (400°) for 30 minutes. Remove aluminum foil and bake 20–30 minutes uncovered or until potatoes are tender and golden brown.

Serve immediately from bakingdish.

Makes 4 servings.

15

Swedish Pancakes with Jam

MARINATED ANCHOVY FILLETS MARINERAD ANSJOVIS

1 can Swedish anchovy fillets (about 18 fillets)
2 tablespoons salad oil
1 tablespoon chopped chives or dill

Drain anchovy fillets; arrange on small serving plate. Pour oil over, and sprinkle with chives or dill. Chill in refrigerator a few hour before serving. Serve on the Smörgåsbord or as an appetizer.

ANCHOVIES PIQUANT PIKANT ANSJOVIS

For those, who love something tangy before dinner this little morsel will be a favorite.

1 can Swedish anchovy fillets (about 18 fillets)
3 tablespoons salad oil
3 tablespoons chopped parsley
3 finely chopped shallots or scallions
1 tablespoon tarragon vinegar

Drain anchovy fillets; place on small serving dish.
Mix remaining ingredients together until a thick paste (if not thick enough add some more onions or parsley).
Pour sauce over anchovies, and marinate for at least 1 hour before serving. Serve on shredded whole wheat crackers, or on the Smörgåsbord.

HERRING AU GRATIN SILLGRATIN

A typically Swedish warm herring dish.

2 salt herring
1/3 cup butter or margarine
2 cups sliced onions
6 medium raw potatoes (about 3 cups)
1 tablespoon fine, dry bread crumbs

Clean herring, removing heads. Rinse under cold running water. Soak in cold water 10–12 hours, changing water a few times so herring will not be

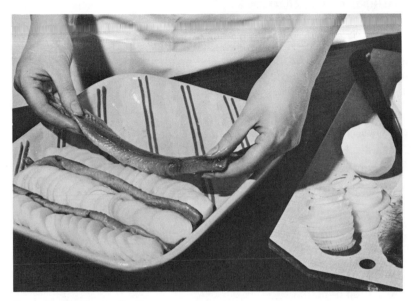

Preparing Herring au Gratin
Beredning av Sillgratin

too salty. You could start the soaking a few hours before going to bed, changing water a few times, and then leaving to soak over night.

Cut herring along backbone. Remove the big backbone and as many small bones as possible; pull off the skin. The bones come out easily after the soaking. Drain fillets on absorbent paper.

Melt half amount of the butter or margarine in skillet and sauté onions over very low heat until they get soft, but not browned.

Peel and slice potatoes thinly.

Butter a shallow 6-cup baking dish with part of the butter. Arrange in it alternate rows of potatoes and onions, with herring between the rows. See color picture of Smörgåsbord between pp. 14 and 15, and picture above.

Sprinkle dry bread crumbs over the dish and dot with remaining butter.

Bake in hot oven (400°) for 20 minutes, covered with aluminum foil, remove foil and bake 20 minutes longer or until potatoes are tender.

Serve immediately from the baking dish.

Makes 4–6 servings.

GOURMET HERRING

Many Americans say they do not go for all the herring that is served in Sweden.
That does not hold true about this dish. I have served it in the States many times as an appetizer along with aquavit or dry martinis, and the herring was always finished well before the drinks were.

4 Matjes herring fillets in wine-flavored sauce
1 cup sour cream or mayonnaise
2 hard-cooked eggs
1/4 cup pickled red beets, chopped
2 tablespoons chopped chives or cucumber

Rinse herring and slice it thinly.
Place cut herring on rectangular serving platter and spread with sour cream or mayonnaise.
Separate egg yolks from egg whites, and chop finely.
Spoon egg yolks, pickled red beets, egg whites and chives or cucumber in rows on top of herring.
Chill a few hours before serving.
Serve on the Smörgåsbord, see color picture between pp. 8 and 9, or as an appetizer with small boiled potatoes.

EGGS WITH CAVIAR

It is quick to make and very piquant served as a dunking sauce with potato chips or as a canapé spread. In Sweden it naturally belongs on the Smörgåsbord.

1/2 cup heavy cream
2-3 tablespoons Swedish caviar
1-2 tablespoons finely chopped onion
2 hard-cooked eggs, sliced
   toast

Whip cream. Fold in caviar and onion to suit your taste. Pile in a mound in center of serving plate.
Arrange egg slices around mound and border with small pieces of fresh toast or crackers.

Stuffed Eggs
Fyllda ägg

STUFFED EGGS   FYLLDA ÄGG

4 hard-cooked eggs
2 tablespoons butter or margarine
5 Swedish anchovy fillets, minced, or 1 tablespoon anchovy paste

Peel eggs and cut in half crosswise, or lengthwise. Remove egg yolks carefully and mix with butter or margarine and anchovies until smooth.

Cut a thin slice from bottom of egg whites so they will stand steadily. Fill with anchovy mixture. Place a small sprig of parsley on top and place on lettuce leaves. Arrange on a platter with slices of tomato, see picture above.

19

EGGS WITH MAYONNAISE AND SHRIMP

RÄKMAJONNÄS

4 hard-cooked eggs
1¹/₂ cups cooked shrimp
1 head of lettuce
¹/₄ cup heavy cream
¹/₄ cup mayonnaise

1 tablespoon chopped dill, chives, or parsley
1-1¹/₂ teaspoons lemon juice
¹/₂ teaspoon salt
dash of pepper

Peel eggs and cut into halves or quarters and arrange on serving dish. Shell shrimp, remove black vein. Place on shredded lettuce leaves around eggs.

Whip the cream. Add mayonnaise, dill, chives or parsley, lemon juice (to taste), salt and pepper. Blend well and dribble over eggs. Or it can be served separately as a sauce with the egg-shrimp dish.

Makes 4 servings.

Omelets

FRENCH OMELET

FRANSK OMELETT

The simplest and quickest form of omelet is the French omelet, which you can serve plain or with an addition of chopped green herbs, such as parsley, chives and dill; or with sliced mushrooms or ham cubes; or plain with a cream sauce as filling, see color picture of Smörgåsbord between pages 14 and 15.

6 large eggs
6 tablespoons water or cream
¹/₂ teaspoon salt
dash of pepper
3 tablespoons butter (preferably no substitute)

The French say that an omelet shall only be beaten 7 strokes. Try, if you can, to make it that way, otherwise beat eggs with water or cream (but no milk), salt and pepper just long enough to mix whites and yolks.

Melt butter in an omelet pan (or in a heavy skillet with round edge) until golden in color and until you can smell its fragrance. At this point pour egg mixture into pan. Shake pan lightly over fire to keep omelet from sticking. As omelet thickens prick with fork so that uncooked mixture can run to the bottom and move sides in towards middle while shaking pan gently.

When omelet is of creamy consistency raise handle and tilt pan so that omelet folds over. Hold pan in this position over the heat a few seconds before letting omelet slide down onto a hot serving platter.

Makes 4 servings.

Fillings for Omelets – added to beaten eggs before cooking.

Green Herbs *(Fines Herbes)* – Add $^1/_4$ cup chopped mixed green herbs such as parsley, chives or dill or any kind of fresh herbs suitable to your taste.

Ham – Add $^1/_2$–$^3/_4$ cup cooked or baked ham cut into small cubes and 2 tablespoons chopped parsley or chives.

Mushrooms – Add $^3/_4$–1 cup sliced sautéed or canned mushrooms.

Creamed Fillings – Spread half amount over omelet before folding and half on the platter around omelet.

Creamed Mushrooms, see below.
Creamed Asparagus, see page 22.
Creamed Sweetbreads, see page 22.
Creamed Lobster, see page 23.
Creamed Spinach, see page 23.

CREAMED MUSHROOMS   SVAMPSTUVNING

$^1/_2$ **pound mushrooms**	**2 tablespoons all-purpose flour**
2 tablespoons butter or margarine	$^1/_2$ **cup cream**
1 tablespoon chopped onion	$^1/_2$ **cup milk**
1 teaspoon salt	$^1/_2$ **teaspoon Worcestershire sauce**
dash of pepper	**1 tablespoon sherry or**
1 teaspoon lemon juice	**dry vermouth, optional**

Slice cleaned mushrooms lengthwise.

Melt butter or margarine in saucepan. Add mushrooms, onion, salt, pepper and lemon juice. Cover and simmer for 5 minutes.

Stir in flour. Gradually add cream, milk and Worcestershire sauce. Cook, stirring, until smooth and thickened. Stir in wine and remove from heat.

Serve as filling in omelet or in pastry shells.

Makes 4 servings.

CREAMED ASPARAGUS

STUVAD SPARRIS

2 tablespoons butter or margarine
3 tablespoons all-purpose flour
1 No. 300 can green asparagus
   spears

$2/3$ cup asparagus liquid
$2/3$ cup cream or milk
$3/4$ teaspoon salt
dash of pepper

Melt butter or margarine in saucepan, add flour and gradually stir in liquid. Cook stirring until smooth, season with salt and pepper.
   Cut asparagus with scissors into small pieces. Save a few for garnish. Add remaining asparagus just before serving.
Makes 4 servings.

CREAMED SWEETBREADS

STUVAD KALVBRÄSS

2 pair sweetbreads (about $13/4$
   pounds)
1 quart boiling water
1 tablespoon salt
1 tablespoon lemon juice
2 tablespoons butter or margarine
2 tablespoons chopped onion
$1/2$ pound sliced mushrooms
   (or 1 3-ounce can)

2 tablespoons all-purpose flour
$3/4$ cup sweetbread stock
$3/4$ cup cream
2 teaspoons salt
$1/8$ teaspoon pepper
2 teaspoons lemon juice
1 tablespoon sherry or
   dry vermouth, optional

Soak sweetbreads in cold water for 1 hour. Drain, place in saucepan and pour boiling water over sweetbreads, add salt and lemon juice, bring to the boiling point and simmer for 20 minutes.
   Remove sweetbreads from stock. Cool stock quickly by putting pan in cold water. Add sweetbreads when stock is cold. Keep them in stock until ready to prepare.
   Trim away membranes and tubes from sweetbreads and cut into 1-inch cubes.
   Melt butter or margarine in saucepan. Add onion and mushrooms; sauté for a few minutes. Stir in flour. Gradually add stock and cream. Cook, stirring until smooth and thickened. Add salt, pepper and lemon juice. Stir in sweetbread cubes and heat slowly. Add wine just before serving.
   Serve in pastry shells, on toast or as an omelet filling.
Makes 4 servings.

CREAMED SPINACH

SPENATSTUVNING

1 pound fresh spinach

or 1 12-ounce package frozen

2 tablespoons butter or margarine

3 tablespoons all-purpose flour

$1/2$-1 cup spinach liquid or milk

1 teaspoon salt

$1/2$ teaspoon lemon juice

$1/4$ teaspoon sugar

Rinse fresh spinach in water; drain.

Put spinach into saucepan and steam over low heat until soft.

Remove spinach, drain well, chop finely or place in electric blender.

Melt butter or margarine, add flour and stir in $1/2$ cup of the liquid; cook until smooth (for a milder flavored and lighter colored cream sauce use milk). Add spinach and seasonings and more liquid if necessary.

Electric Blender Method:

Place spinach with $1/2$ cup of liquid and balance of ingredients in container, turn on motor. Turn off and scrape down a few times until spinach is completely puréed. Pour purée into saucepan and cook a few minutes – adding more liquid if necessary.

Use for filling in omelet or serve with fried fish dishes.

Makes 4 servings.

CREAMED LOBSTER

HUMMERSTUVNING

1 5-ounce can lobster

2 tablespoons butter or margarine

2 tablespoons all-purpose flour

$1/4$ cup lobster liquid

$1^1/3$ cups cream or milk

$3/4$-1 teaspoon salt

dash of cayenne

Drain lobster saving $1/4$ cup of the liquid for use in sauce. Cut lobster meat into small pieces.

Melt butter or margarine; blend in flour until smooth. Gradually add lobster liquid and cream, stirring constantly. Simmer for a few minutes.

Remove from heat; add lobster, salt and cayenne. Reheat quickly (if lobster is cooked too long, it gets tough and chewy).

Serve as omelet filling, or in pastry shells.

You may substitute shrimp, crabmeat or crayfish for lobster.

Makes 4 servings.

OMELET AU GRATIN

An excellent omelet which has an advantage over other kinds because it can be prepared ahead of time. It is a filled French Omelet with a cheese sauce on top. It makes good eating, served with crisp bacon or sliced, cooked ham and a salad.

Filling:

1 pound fresh spinach
   or 1 12-ounce package frozen
1 tablespoon butter or margarine
$1/2$ teaspoon salt

Cheese Sauce:

1 tablespoon all-purpose flour
$11/2$ cups cream or top milk
$1/4$ cup grated Parmesan cheese
$1/2$ teaspoon salt
   dash of pepper

Omelet:

6 large eggs
4 tablespoons cream
2 tablespoons water
$1/2$ teaspoon salt
   dash of pepper
2 tablespoons butter (preferably no substitute)

Topping:

$1/4$ cup grated Parmesan cheese

Filling:

Rinse fresh spinach in water; drain.

Steam in its own liquid until soft. Drain off liquid *very well*. (Do the same if using frozen spinach.) Add butter or margarine and salt, toss lightly and set aside.

Cheese Sauce

Beat flour into cream or top milk in a small saucepan. Place pan over heat and let come to the boiling point, while stirring; cook slowly 10 minutes. Add cheese and taste sauce before adding salt and pepper. Sometimes cheese contains enough salt in itself.

Omelet

Beat eggs, cream, water, salt and pepper just enough to mix together.

Melt butter in an omelet pan (or in a heavy skillet) until golden brown in color. Pour egg mixture into pan and shake it gently over heat to keep it from sticking. Prick with fork so that uncooked mixture can penetrate. Keep on shaking pan until omelet has an even creamy consistency.

Spread omelet with *well drained* spinach. Raise handle to tilt pan to make omelet fold over; slide omelet onto a buttered fire-proof platter.

Spoon Cheese Sauce over omelet, top with grated cheese.

Bake in hot oven (425°) 10 minutes or broil (with top of omelet 5–6 inches from heat) until golden brown.

(If you have prepared omelet ahead of time it is better to bake it so it gets heated through properly.)

Instead of spinach, sautéed mushrooms, asparagus tips or cubed, baked ham can be used as a filling.

Makes 4 servings.

VELVETY OMELET WITH
CREAMED ASPARAGUS JUBILEUMSOMELETT

A nice decorative egg dish with many varieties, which is easy to make. It can be made in a loaf pan as well as in a ring mold, whichever is more suitable, and may be served with any kind of creamed sauces.

$2^2/_3$ cups milk
6 eggs, beaten
1 teaspoon salt   *Garnish:*
  dash of pepper   1 cup cooked, peeled shrimp
Creamed Asparagus, see recipe,   1 tablespoon chopped parsley
  page 22   or dill

Pour milk into saucepan, bring to a boil and pour over beaten eggs; add salt and pepper.

Butter a $9^1/_2 \times 5^1/_4 \times 2^3/_4$-inch loaf pan (or a 5-cup ring mold); pour egg mixture into pan.

Cover with buttered waxed paper and tie with string or with aluminum foil.

Place pan in a small roasting pan filled with hot water.

Bake in moderate oven (350°) 40–50 minutes or until a knife inserted in the middle comes out clean.

Remove waxed paper and unmold omelet on warm serving platter.

Cut loaf-shaped omelet in thick slices, arrange shrimp in a row on top, sprinkle with parsley or dill. Spoon Creamed Asparagus on both sides of omelet.

Garnish with a few asparagus spears.

Serve as is or with sliced cooked ham and Tomato Salad, see page 83.

Makes 5–6 servings.

FLUFFY OMELET

5 eggs, separated
$2/3$ cup cream
$2/3$ cup milk
  dash of pepper
$1/2$ teaspoon salt

Butter generously a shallow 1-quart baking dish (with round bottom) or an omelet pan with fire-proof handle.

Mix egg yolks with cream, milk and pepper.

Beat egg whites with salt until they hold stiff but moist peaks.

Fold egg whites into egg yolk mixture and pour into baking dish.

Bake in moderate oven (350°) 20 minutes or until high and fluffy and golden brown.

Pour Creamed Filling, see page 21, over omelet in baking dish or invert omelet on large buttered lid. Slide half of omelet onto a hot serving platter, pour filling over this part of omelet and fold the other half over. Pour additional creamed sauce around omelet and garnish with parsley and some tomato slices.

Makes 4 servings.

BAKED OMELET WITH
CREAMED SAUCE

4 eggs
$3/4$ teaspoon salt
  dash of pepper
1 cup milk

Beat eggs slightly; add salt, pepper and milk; blend well. Pour into buttered 8-inch pie plate or shallow casserole dish. Bake in moderate oven (350°) until firm and golden brown, about 25 minutes.

Prepare a filling of creamed vegetables (such as asparagus, spinach or mushrooms), or Creamed Lobster or Creamed Sweetbreads, see pages 23 and 22.

When omelet is baked, pour creamed sauce over omelet.

Makes 4 servings.

EGGS AU GRATIN

GRATINERADE ÄGG

A good dish on the Smörgåsbord or for supper with cold, sliced ham.

1 pound fresh spinach
1 teaspoon salt
2 tablespoons butter or margarine
3 tablespoons grated Parmesan
    cheese
4 eggs

Cheese Sauce:
3 tablespoons butter or margarine
3 tablespoons all-purpose flour
2 cups top milk
$1/3$ cup grated Parmesan cheese
1 egg yolk, beaten
    dash of pepper
$1/2 - 3/4$ teaspoon salt
1 tablespoon fine, dry bread crumbs

Rinse spinach in water; drain.

Put into saucepan with salt, steam until tender (5-8 minutes), drain well. Add butter or margarine and toss lightly.

Place spinach in bottom of buttered, deep $1^1/_2$-quart baking dish.

Make 4 shallow indentations in spinach with back of tablespoon, sprinkle these with cheese.

Break eggs, pour carefully into hollows.

Cheese Sauce:

Melt butter or margarine, stir in flour and blend well. Gradually add milk, stirring until smooth.

Add cheese and simmer sauce 2-3 minutes, remove pan from heat.

Beat in egg yolk and pepper, taste sauce before adding salt (amount depends upon saltiness of cheese).

Spoon sauce over eggs and spinach, sprinkle with bread crumbs.

Bake in hot oven (425°) 8-10 minutes or until golden brown and bubbly.

Makes 4 servings.

BAKED HAM OMELET

SKINKLÅDA

This is a good dish to serve for Sunday lunch. Very easy to prepare too.

Prepare omelet as in Baked Omelet with Creamed Sauce, see page 26, but omit the salt.

Add **1 cup cubed cooked smoked ham** and **1 tablespoon chopped chives** to egg mixture. Bake as in Baked Omelet with Creamed Sauce, page 26.

Soufflés

MUSHROOM SOUFFLÉ

SVAMPSUFFLÉ

A wonderful dish, light and flavorful. Can be prepared in advance, with the exception of beating the egg whites. Please follow the instructions carefully.

$1/2$ pound fresh or 2 4-ounce cans mushrooms

2 tablespoons butter or margarine

3 tablespoons all-purpose flour

1 cup milk

$1/4$ cup cream

3 egg yolks

$3/4$ cup egg whites (about 5 egg whites)

$3/4$ teaspoon salt

dash of pepper

1 tablespoon dry vermouth

Wipe off sand from mushrooms with damp paper towel.

Chop finely and sauté in butter or margarine for about 5 minutes. Season mushrooms with a few drops of lemon juice and salt.

Dust mushrooms with flour and add milk and cream, stirring constantly. Cook stirring, until smooth and thick, remove from heat.

Beat egg yolks and add to cream sauce, beating vigorously. Place over heat for a few minutes until sauce thickens, but do not cook. Remove from heat and add salt, pepper and dry vermouth; cool.

Beat egg whites until they hold stiff peaks.

Fold egg whites into creamed sauce.

Pour mixture into an unbuttered $1^1/_2$ quart deep baking dish or into a soufflé pan.

Bake in slow oven (325°) 55–60 minutes or until middle of soufflé is firm. Serve immediately with melted butter. If you have to wait a few minutes, turn off heat, leaving soufflé in oven.

Served as a first course instead of a soup for dinner the soufflé will serve 5, but as a luncheon dish (and it is a most luscious one), it will not make more than 3 servings.

VEGETABLE SOUFFLÉ

GRÖNSAKSSUFFLÉ

$1^1/_2$ cups cooked vegetables

2 tablespoons butter or margarine

3 tablespoons all-purpose flour

1 cup milk

$1/4$ cup cream

3 egg yolks

$3/4$ cup egg whites (about 5 egg whites)

1 teaspoon salt

dash of pepper

dash of nutmeg

Vegetables:
Use cauliflower, asparagus or broccoli. Vegetables should be cooked in slightly salted water until almost done, then drained and cooled. Cauliflower should be broken into very small flowerets; asparagus and broccoli cut into small pieces.

To make the soufflé:
Melt butter or margarine in a heavy saucepan; blend in flour; gradually add milk and cream, stirring constantly. Cook, stirring, until smooth and thick. Remove from heat.

Beat egg yolks. Add to cream sauce, beating vigorously. Place over heat for a few minutes until sauce thickens, but do not cook. Remove from heat and add salt, pepper and nutmeg. Cool.

Stir vegetables gently into sauce.

Beat egg whites until they hold stiff peaks. Fold them carefully into vegetable mixture.

Pour mixture into an unbuttered $1^1/_2$ quart deep baking dish and bake in slow oven (325°) 55–60 minutes or until firm.

Serve immediately with melted butter or Hollandaise Sauce, see page 165. If you have to wait a few minutes, turn off heat and leave soufflé in the oven.

Served as first course with a dinner the soufflé will serve 5, but as a luncheon dish, it will not make more than 3 servings.

FISH SOUFFLÉ   FISKSUFFLÉ

$1/_4$ cup butter or margarine	2 teaspoons salt
$1/_3$ cup all-purpose flour	$1/_8$ teaspoon pepper
$1^1/_2$ cups milk	1 tablespoon butter or margarine
4 eggs, separated	2 tablespoons fine, dry bread
2 cups boiled flaked fish	crumbs

Melt butter or margarine in saucepan. Blend in flour. Gradually stir in milk. Cook, stirring, until smooth and thickened. Remove from heat.

Beat egg yolks with a little of the sauce; pour into sauce, beating vigorously.

Add fish, salt and pepper to sauce. Let mixture cool.

Beat egg whites until stiff. Fold into fish mixture.

Butter a 2 quart deep baking dish and coat with bread crumbs. Pour fish mixture into dish and bake in slow oven (325°) until set, about $1-1^1/_4$ hours.

Serve immediately from baking dish with Lobster Sauce, see page 166, Mushroom Sauce, see page 164, or Hollandaise Sauce, see page 165.

Makes 4 servings.

FILLED PANCAKES FYLLDA PANNKAKOR

These pancakes are wonderful as a hors d'œuvre or as a simple meal. They are easy to serve, when company comes, because the pancakes can be cooked and filled ahead of time – just sprinkle with cheese, dot with butter and heat at serving time.

Two kinds of fillings have been included, so that you can choose, whichever you like best.

Batter:

3 eggs, slightly beaten

$1^1/_3$ cups sifted all-purpose flour

$^1/_2$ teaspoon salt

$2^1/_4$ cups milk

$^3/_4$ cup cream

$^1/_4$ cup melted butter or margarine

Filling I:

1 pound fresh or frozen cooked
   shrimp

2 tablespoons fresh dill or chives

$^1/_4$ cup butter or margarine

2 tablespoons all-purpose flour

$^1/_2$ cup heavy cream

$^1/_2$ cup milk

1 egg yolk, slightly beaten

1 tablespoon sherry or
   dry vermouth

$^1/_4$–$^3/_4$ teaspoon salt

1 tablespoon lemon juice

Filling II:

$^1/_2$ pound mushrooms

2 tablespoons chopped onion

3 tablespoons butter or margarine

2 tablespoons all-purpose flour

1 cup cream

1 tablespoon sherry or
   dry vermouth

1 teaspoon salt

$^1/_4$ teaspoon pepper

Topping:

$^1/_2$ cup grated Parmesan cheese

2 tablespoons butter or margarine

Batter:

Beat eggs slightly in mixing bowl. Combine flour and salt. Add to egg mixture all at once. Stir in milk and cream gradually. Beat mixture until well blended. Add melted butter.

Filling I:

Shell shrimp, remove black vein. Cut into small pieces, sprinkle with dill and refrigerate.

Melt butter or margarine in top of double boiler over low heat. Blend in flour. Gradually stir in cream and milk. Cook, stirring constantly, over boiling water until thick. Remove from heat.

Beat in egg yolk, sherry or dry vermouth, salt, lemon juice and shrimp.

Filling of Pancakes
Fyllning av pannkakor

Filling II:
Prepare as in Creamed Mushrooms, see page 21.

To make filled pancakes:
These pancakes are cooked one at a time and should measure about 6 inches in diameter. Use preferably a small, 6-inch frying pan or a griddle.

Heat frying pan to medium hot; add a very small amount of melted butter. Beat batter slightly to be sure it's well mixed and pour 3 tablespoons into pan; tilting pan to spread out batter, and to make a 6-inch circle. Brown lightly, about 1 minute on each side. Remove from pan, spread 1 tablespoon filling across center. Roll up and place on oven-proof platter, see picture above. Repeat until all batter has been used.

Sprinkle filled, rolled pancakes with grated cheese. Dot with butter. Bake in hot oven (425°) until cheese melts and pancakes are hot, about 10–12 minutes.

Makes 4–6 servings.

31

CHEESE SOUFFLÉ

2 tablespoons butter or margarine
3 tablespoons all-purpose flour
1 cup milk
3 egg yolks

1 cup grated Cheddar cheese,
firmly packed
$1/4$–1 teaspoon salt
dash of pepper
$3/4$–1 cup egg whites (about 5–6
egg whites)

Melt butter or margarine in saucepan. Blend in flour. Gradually stir in milk. Cook, stirring, until smooth and thick (sauce should pull away from side of pan). Remove from heat.

Beat egg yolks well. Add to sauce, beating vigorously. Blend in cheese. Taste sauce before adding salt – sometimes cheese is quite salty. Add salt to taste and pepper.

Beat egg whites first on low speed until foamy. Then turn up speed to high and continue to beat until stiff peaks form. Fold carefully into cheese mixture. Pour into an unbuttered $1^1/2$ quart deep baking dish.

Bake in slow oven (325°) until set, about 50–60 minutes. Serve immediately. If soufflé has to wait a few minutes, leave in oven, but turn off heat.

Makes 4 servings.

LOBSTER SOUFFLÉ

This soufflé is extremely delicate and very easy to make.
Serve it as a luncheon dish or as an appetizer. If you wish to make the meal more filling, serve the soufflé with Hollandaise Sauce.

1 5-ounce can lobster or crab
meat (1 cup firmly packed)
4 eggs, separated
3 tablespoons butter or margarine
3 tablespoons all-purpose flour
1 cup cream
$1/4$ cup lobster liquid

1 tablespoon dry vermouth,
optional
$3/4$ teaspoon salt
dash of cayenne

Drain lobster but save the liquid for use in sauce. Cut lobster into small pieces. Beat egg yolks slightly

Melt butter or margarine; blend in flour. Gradually add cream and lobster liquid stirring constantly. Cook, stirring, until sauce is smooth. Reduce heat and stir in egg yolks, beating vigorously. Cook 2–3 minutes more, stirring constantly, until sauce thickens to consistency of mayonnaise. Do not allow it to boil. Remove from heat and stir in lobster meat, vermouth, salt and cayenne. Blend well and let cool.

Beat egg whites until stiff; fold gently into cooled lobster mixture.

Pour mixture into an unbuttered $1^1/_2$ quart deep casserole or soufflé mold; or into small individual casseroles, filling them to within $^1/_4$-inch from the top.

Place soufflé on center rack of a slow oven (325°) and bake until lightly browned and firm, about 50–60 minutes and 15–18 minutes for individual ones. For best results, don't open oven door during baking or your soufflé may fall. Serve at once with melted butter to which a few drops of lemon juice has been added.

Makes 2 servings as a main course or 4 as an appetizer.

CREAMED EGGS WITH CHEESE AND FRANKFURTERS

STUVADE ÄGG MED PRINSKORV OCH ROSTAT BRÖD

6 hard-cooked eggs	$^1/_4$ pound sharp American process cheese, cut up
3 tablespoons butter or margarine	$^1/_2$ teaspoon salt
3 tablespoons all-purpose flour	dash of pepper
$^1/_3$ cup cream	1 tablespoon chopped parsley
$1^1/_4$ cups milk (about)	8 frankfurters
	4 slices white bread

Use one of the eggs for garnish. Chop yolks and whites separately.

Cut remaining eggs into quarters.

Melt butter or margarine, blend in flour. Add cream slowly; cook, stirring constantly. Add milk to make a smooth, rather thin sauce. Stir in cheese, salt and pepper.

Cover pan and simmer, without stirring, over low heat until cheese melts, 10–15 minutes.

Stir to blend and add quartered eggs. Bring sauce to the boiling point. (If sauce gets too thick, add a little more milk.)

Split frankfurters, and cut in halves; fry or broil until crisp and brown.

Toast bread slices. Cut into triangles.

Pour creamed eggs onto hot serving platter. Garnish with rows of chopped egg yolk, egg white, and parsley. Poke frankfurters part way into egg mixture around the edge of dish, alternately with toast triangles.

Makes 4 servings.

4

Shaping meatballs with hand and tablespoon

Köttbullar formas för hand med hjälp av sked

Shaping meatballs with pastry bag and knife

Köttbullar formas med hjälp av strut och kniv

34

Small Meatballs   Små köttbullar

SMALL MEATBALLS   SMÅ KÖTTBULLAR

One never gets tired of these; serve them on tooth picks with cocktails, cold on sandwiches, or as the Swedish people do, on the Smörgåsbord.

$^1/_4$ cup finely chopped onion $^1/_4$ pound ground, lean pork

1 tablespoon shortening   2 teaspoons salt

$^1/_4$ cup fine, dry bread crumbs $^1/_4$ teaspoon pepper

$^1/_3$ cup water   dash of cloves

$^1/_3$ cup cream $^1/_3$ cup butter or margarine

$^3/_4$ pound ground beef (round steak) $^1/_4$ cup of boiling water

For best meatballs select meat yourself and have it ground. The fresher the meat is ground, the better meatballs.

Sauté onion in shortening until golden brown.

Soak crumbs in water-cream mixture.

Combine onion, crumb mixture, meats and seasonings. Mix thoroughly until smooth. Shape into small balls with palm of your hand (wet your hands before handling meat so it won't stick) using a teaspoon dipped in cold water; or press through a pastry bag, see pictures beside.

Fry in butter or margarine until evenly brown, shaking pan continuously to make balls round; add boiling water, cover and simmer 5–10 minutes or until tender. Makes 70 small meatballs.

KIDNEY SAUTÉ

4 veal kidneys (about 1¹/₂ pounds)
1 tablespoon butter or margarine
1 4-ounce can mushrooms
1¹/₂ teaspoons salt
¹/₈ teaspoon pepper
2 tablespoons all-purpose flour

1 cup beef bouillon, mushroom
  liquid or water
¹/₂ cup cream or milk
1 tablespoon sherry or
  dry vermouth

Soak kidneys in cold water for 1 hour. Drain. Place in saucepan and cover with cold water. Place over low heat and let water slowly come to the boiling point. Drain and rinse in cold water. Remove heavy veins and part of fat from kidneys; cut into ¹/₂-inch slices.

Brown butter or margarine in skillet. Add kidneys and brown quickly. If there seems to be too much fat, pour some of it off.

Add mushrooms, salt and pepper; brown for a few minutes. Sprinkle flour over mixture. Gradually stir in bouillon, mushroom liquid, or water; add cream. Cover and cook over low heat 10 minutes. Remove from heat and add sherry or vermouth.

Makes 4 servings.

ONION CASSEROLE

2 tablespoons butter or margarine
4 cups sliced onions
¹/₂ pound ground pork
¹/₂ pound ground veal or beef
¹/₄ cup fine dry bread crumbs

1¹/₄ cups milk
1 teaspoon salt
¹/₄ teaspoon pepper
¹/₂ cup stock (¹/₂ bouillon cube
  dissolved in ¹/₂ cup water)

Melt butter or margarine in frying pan. Add onions and sauté until golden brown.

Mix meats, bread crumbs, milk and seasonings. Combine thoroughly until smooth.

Turn half of onions into a shallow 6-cup casserole and cover with meat mixture; top with remaining onions. Pour in stock, making holes in mixture to let it run down.

Bake in moderate oven (375°) 25–30 minutes. At about half baking time, check to see if top of dish is getting too brown; cover if necessary.

Serve hot as part of Smörgåsbord, or as a supper dish with baked potatoes and green salad.

Makes 4–5 servings.

SAUTÉED MUSHROOMS   STEKT SVAMP

1 pound mushrooms
3 tablespoons butter or margarine
1 tablespoon chopped onion
1 teaspoon salt
  dash of pepper
$1/2$ teaspoon lemon juice

Wipe mushrooms with a damp paper towel or rinse quickly under running cold water.
Melt butter or margarine in frying pan. Add onion and sauté for a few minutes; add mushrooms. Stir in salt, pepper and lemon juice. Sauté over low heat until soft and golden brown, about 10–15 minutes.
Serve on the Smörgåsbord, or with meat or fish.
Makes 4 servings.

SHRIMP-SALMON ASPIC

ALADÅB PÅ LAX
OCH RÄKOR

1 11-ounce can chicken consommé	$2^1/_4$ cups cold water
6 peppercorns	1 cup cooked shrimp
6 whole allspice	1 hard-cooked egg, sliced
1 bay leaf	2 cups flaked salmon, mackerel
6 sprigs of fresh dill	or eel
2 envelopes unflavored gelatin	1 cup diced celery

Place chicken consommé in saucepan.
Put in a bag of cheesecloth the peppercorns, allspice, bay leaf and dill. Place in saucepan and simmer 10 minutes; remove spicebag.
Soften gelatin in $1/_4$ cup water and dissolve mixture in hot consommé.
Add the 2 cups of cold water and chill until thick and syrupy.
Arrange the shrimp in a $1^1/_2$-quart, $9^3/_4$-inch ring mold.
Spoon half of gelatin gently over shrimp; chill until almost firm.
Stand the egg slices upright in the gelatin layer.
Spoon more gelatin over eggs; chill.
Then add salmon, mackerel or eel and celery.
Add remaining gelatin, chill until firm. Turn out on large platter; fill center with lettuce.
Makes 6–8 servings.

Preparing Stuffed Onions
Beredning av lökdolmar

STUFFED ONIONS

LÖKDOLMAR

A tasty economical dish.

8 medium onions	2 tablespoons butter or margarine
Veal Meatballs, see recipe, page 67	$^3/_4$ cup onion liquid

Peel onions and boil in slightly salted water 10 minutes. Drain, reserving $^3/_4$ cup liquid.

When onions are cool, make a cut from side of onion just to the center; separate natural onion layers to get hollow onion "shells".

Place a teaspoon of veal meatball mixture inside each "shell". The shells will shape themselves around the meat and will stay there without tying; see picture above.

Melt butter or margarine in skillet; add stuffed onion shells and cook 10–15 minutes, or until nicely browned. Add onion stock; cover and simmer for 20 minutes.

Serve on the Smörgåsbord.

Makes 4 servings.

38

FILLED BAKED TOMATOES

These are nice to make if you have leftover ham, rice or spaghetti.

10 large tomatoes
1 tablespoon shortening
$3/4$ cup chopped onions
1 cup cooked ham or mixed
   luncheon meat
1 cup cooked rice or spaghetti
$1^1/2$ teaspoons all-purpose flour

$3/4$ cup sour cream
2 teaspoons Soya sauce
   dash of pepper
2 tablespoons chopped chives or
   parsley
1 tablespoon grated cheese
1 tablespoon fine dry bread crumbs

Cut off a thin slice from top of tomatoes, scoop out pulp.

Melt shortening in frying pan, add onions and sauté for 5 minutes. Chop ham or luncheon meat and add to onions, cook stirring occasionally until onions are soft.

Stir in rice or spaghetti, flour, sour cream, Soya sauce, pepper and chives or parsley. Let cook a few minutes. Season to taste with salt.

Stuff tomatoes with mixture, place in buttered baking dish.

Sprinkle with cheese and bread crumbs.

Bake in moderate oven (375°) 15–20 minutes or until golden brown.

Makes 4 servings.

(Use tomato pulp to make Clear Tomato Soup, see page 66.)

CAULIFLOWER WITH CREAMED SHRIMP

A very popular summer dish in Sweden, decorative too.

1 large head cauliflower
   boiling water
   salt

Cream Sauce:
2 tablespoons butter or margarine
2 tablespoons all-purpose flour
1 cup milk

1 cup cream
$1/2$–1 teaspoon salt
   dash of Cayenne
2 tablespoons chopped dill or
   parsley
$1^1/2$ cups cooked, peeled shrimp
2 tablespoons dry vermouth,
   optional

Cauliflower with Creamed Shrimp
Blomkål med räkstuvning

Cut off tough end of stem, remove leaves and soak in cold, salted water with head down for 10–15 minutes.

Drain cauliflower break into 4 large flowerets. Place head up in large saucepan. Add boiling water and let come to the boiling point. Reduce heat and simmer, covered until barely tender (about 10 minutes).

For cream sauce, melt butter or margarine, stir in flour and add milk and cream. Simmer sauce until smooth and thickened.

Season with $1/_2$ teaspoon salt, (add eventually more salt after you have added shrimp) cayenne, chopped dill or parsley and 1 cup cut-up shrimp.

Remove pan from heat, add vermouth, if so desired, and pour sauce into a shallow round or square, hot serving dish.

Drain cauliflower and stick into sauce, arranging remaining shrimp, cut lengthwise, around cauliflower, see picture above.

If you have to keep the dish warm for some time, cover with foil and place in slow oven.

Makes 4 servings.

HAM AU GRATIN WITH LEEK
OR BELGIAN ENDIVE

PURJULÖKSLÅDA

8 medium thick leeks or	$1/2$ cup grated Parmesan cheese
8 small Belgian endives	$1/2$ teaspoon salt
8 large slices cooked ham	1 egg yolk
(not too thin)	2 tablespoons cream

Cheese Sauce:

Topping:

2 tablespoons butter or margarine	2 tablespoons grated cheese
3 tablespoons all-purpose flour	2 tablespoons melted butter or
$1^3/4$ cups top milk	margarine

If you are not used to handling leeks remember that they contain a lot of sand between the leaves. Therefore make a split lengthwise and separate leaves carefully while rinsing under running water.

Trim leeks and remove dark green part leaving a piece as long as ham is wide. Cook in small amount of salted water, until completely tender, about 20 minutes. Remove from pan and *drain very well.*

If you use Belgian endive, just wash and place in cold water.

Endive is often slightly bitter; if you object to the bitter taste, hollow out about $1/_2$ inch from the base. Cook in plenty of water for 20 minutes or until completely tender. *Drain very well.* (You might need to squeeze them gently with a paper towel.)

Roll each stalk of leek or endive into ham lengthwise.

Place in buttered oblong baking dish, cover with cheese sauce.

Cheese Sauce:

Melt butter or margarine, add flour and stir until well blended. Add gradually milk; cook stirring until smooth.

Mix in cheese and taste before adding more salt (amount of salt depends on saltiness of cheese).

Remove from heat and beat in egg yolk and cream, mixed together.

Spoon sauce over ham and vegetables until completely covered.
Sprinkle with cheese and brush surface with melted butter or margarine.
(So far dish can be prepared ahead of time.)
Bake in hot oven (400°) 12–15 minutes or until golden brown.
Remove from oven and let stand 5 minutes before serving.
Makes 4 servings.

41

RICE RING WITH CREAMED MUSHROOMS AND BACON

RISRAND MED
SVAMPSTUVNING
OCH BACON

A festive looking dish on the Smörgåsbord, but also suitable for many other occasions.

2 tablespoons shortening
1 cup rice
1/2 teaspoon salt
2 cups water
Creamed Mushrooms, see recipe, page 21
8 slices bacon
2 medium tomatoes
1 tablespoon chopped parsley
   paprika

Melt shortening in small heavy saucepan.

Add rice and salt; stir for a few minutes, pour in water and bring to the boiling point.

Cover pan with buttered waxed paper, place lid on top of waxed paper.

Simmer over very low heat for 18 minutes.

Prepare, in the meantime, Creamed Mushrooms.

Broil or fry bacon until crisp; drain.

Cut tomatoes into sections.

Spoon rice onto a hot serving platter and shape into ring. Fill center with Creamed Mushrooms, arrange bacon alternatively with tomatoes around ring, sprinkle mushrooms with parsley and rice ring with paprika.

Makes 4 servings.

Salads

WEST COAST SALAD   VÄSTKUSTSALLAD

The Swedish West Coast is famous for its variety of good, fresh seafood and it has given its name to this unusual and delicious salad.

There is nothing set about this salad recipe; you can easily add and deduct ingredients after your own taste and economy. But have in mind that mushrooms will loose their flavor and crispness if marinated too long.

In Sweden this salad is served as an appetizer with toasted bread and butter. It is an attractive way to start a dinner.

1/2 pound mushrooms
1 pound cooked shrimp
1 1/2 cup crab meat
1 cup cut-up canned asparagus spears
1 cup sliced celery
1 cup cooked peas
1 small head of lettuce, shredded

Dressing:
1 clove garlic, crushed
4 tablespoons good vinegar
8 tablespoons salad oil
1 1/4 teaspoons salt   *Garnish:*
1 teaspoon paprika   2 hard cooked eggs, sliced
   freshly ground pepper   3 tomatoes, peeled and sliced

Clean mushrooms, slice lengthwise, sprinkle with a few drops lemon juice and keep in covered bowl in refrigerator.

Peel shrimp, leave whole or cut lengthwise. Dice crabmeat and keep with shrimp in refrigerator until serving time. For dressing place all ingredients into a jar, cover and shake until well blended.

Half an hour before serving time assemble all ingredients for salad, place in layers in salad bowl, rubbed with garlic (optional). Pour dressing over and toss lightly.

Garnish bowl with rows of eggs and tomatoes. Chill until serving.

Salad can also be served from a large platter and makes a very attractive looking dish. Place a few lettuce leaves in the middle of platter. Pile salad up high in center on top of leaves and place garnish around in groups or rows.

Makes 5–6 servings.

LOBSTER SALAD

1 small head of lettuce
2 cups cut-up lobster, crabmeat
  or shrimp
1 cup cut-up cooked asparagus or
  canned, sliced mushrooms
1 cup canned, very fine peas
$1/2$ cup finely sliced celery
1 tablespoon chopped dill or parsley

Dressing:
$3/4$ cup mayonnaise
$1/2$ cup heavy cream, whipped
4 teaspoons lemon juice
$1/2$ teaspoon prepared mustard
$1/2$ teaspoon paprika
$3/4$ teaspoon curry
  salt

Line a bowl with lettuce leaves, placing salad ingredients in layers on top. Toss lightly with two forks.

Exact measurement for the dressing is hard to give because brands of mayonnaise differ. The mixture should be liquid enough to run through salad.

Mix mayonnaise with whipped cream and slowly add seasonings to suit your own taste.

Pour dressing over ingredients in bowl, poke lightly with fork, so it can penetrate to the bottom of bowl. Place in refrigerator.

Garnish before serving with a few pieces of the redest part of the lobster.

Serve on the Smörgåsbord or as an hors d'œuvres with buttered slices of thin toast. See color picture of Smörgåsbord between pages 14 and 15.

CHICKEN IN CURRY MAYONNAISE

Chicken and curry is a favorite combination in Sweden. When you have leftover chicken or turkey try this salad.

$2-2^1/2$ cups diced, cooked chicken
  or turkey
1 cup diced, peeled apple
1 cup diced celery
1 tablespoon chopped dill, optional

Curry Mayonnaise:
$1^1/2-2$ teaspoons curry
$3/4$ cup mayonnaise
1 tablespoon lemon juice
  pinch of sugar
$1/2$ cup heavy cream, whipped

Garnish:
2 hard-cooked eggs
1 large tomato

Mix dry ingredients in large salad bowl.

Stir 1¹/₂ teaspoons curry into mayonnaise, add lemon juice and pinch of sugar. Check seasoning, before adding more curry to taste.

Fold in cream.

Spoon curry mayonnaise over salad and toss lightly. Chill thoroughly before serving.

Peel eggs and slice. Cut tomato into wedges.

Garnish salad with alternating egg rings and tomato wedges.

Makes 6 servings.

FRUIT MAYONNAISE

¹/₂ cup heavy cream, whipped	**¹/₂ cup finely diced celery**
¹/₄ cup mayonnaise	**¹/₄ cup chopped walnuts, optional**
1–2 tablespoons lemon juice	**1 9-ounce can crushed pineapple,**
1 cup peeled, finely diced apples	**drained**
2 bananas, finely diced	**¹/₄ pound seedless grapes**

Mix whipped cream and mayonnaise. Season to taste with lemon juice. Add remaining ingredients and toss with forks until evenly blended; chill. Spoon into serving bowl, garnish with green leaves and blue grapes. Serve on the Smörgåsbord.

TOMATO RING

3 large onions	**¹/₈ teaspoon pepper**
2 pounds tomatoes (about 8	**2 envelopes unflavored gelatin**
medium size tomatoes)	**¹/₄ cup cold water**
1 10¹/₂-ounce can consommé	**1 tablespoon butter or margarine**
2 teaspoons salt	**2 tablespoons all-purpose flour**
2 teaspoons sugar	**¹/₄ cup heavy cream**

Peel and slice onions and tomatoes. Place in a saucepan together with consommé and seasonings. Bring mixture to the boiling point and cook, covered, over low heat for 45 minutes, or until vegetables are completely tender. Force through a fine sieve.

Sprinkle gelatin into cold water; let stand a few minutes.

Melt butter or margarine in a saucepan. Add flour and stir until well blended. Gradually add tomato purée; cook and stir until smooth. Add softened gelatin. Remove from heat and taste to check seasoning. Beat in heavy cream.

Brush a 6-cup ring mold with oil and pour in gelatin mixture. Chill until firm.

Loosen ring from mold and invert on round serving platter. Garnish with watercress and serve with slices of boiled ham as part of Smörgåsbord or as a luncheon dish.

Makes 5–6 servings.

GOOD LUNCHEON SALAD   GOD LUNCHSALLAD

This unusual salad is decorative and not expensive. Wonderful when you have leftover meat and potatoes.

Salad:
2 cups finely chopped, cooked potatoes
2 cups finely chopped cooked ham, chicken or hot dogs
2 cups shredded lettuce
1¹/₂ cups chopped or shredded cucumber

Dressing:
6 tablespoons salad oil
3 tablespoons good vinegar

³/₄ teaspoon salt
1 teaspoon paprika
1 teaspoon prepared mustard
1 clove garlic, crushed

Garnish:
1 small head of lettuce
4 hard-cooked eggs
2 tablespoons mayonnaise
2 tablespoons catsup
¹/₄ cup capers, optional

Place salad ingredients in large bowl.

Shake dressing together in covered jar, remove garlic.

Pour over salad; toss lightly.

Arrange lettuce to cover bottom of large round or square serving platter. Spoon salad in the middle and pile it up high.

Peel and halve eggs. Place with cut side down on lettuce, around salad mound. Spread eggs alternatively with mayonnaise and catsup, sprinkle with capers.

Serve cold on the Smörgåsbord or as a luncheon dish.

Makes 4 servings.

46

STARTING AT THE TOP, FROM LEFT TO RIGHT:

Cooked sliced potatoes, dipped in salad dressing, topped with chopped chives, herring-tidbits and sour cream.

Swedish anchovies-sprats and a tomato slice spread with mayonnaise and topped with egg.

Chopped egg yolk and egg white, tomato paste and Swedish anchovies-sprats.

Portuguese sardine with egg and tomato sections.

Smoked salmon with dill and lettuce.

Boiled ham, pineapple, maraschino cherry and lettuce.

Mayonnaise, shrimp, dill and cucumber.

Sliced meatballs with parsley and cocktail onions.

Double sandwich filled with sliced, smoked toungue and creamed liver pâté. Garnished with red currant jelly and celery tops.

Roast beef with horseradish flavored sour cream, strips of leek.

Edam cheese with lettuce and grapes.

Sliced Camembert with radishes.

Cocktail Canapés

In the color picture opposite page 46 and in the black-and-white pictures on page 50, we show you ideas from the modern Swedish kitchen for a cocktail party.

The Swedish people entertain in a more formal style than the Americans do. They put a lot of emphasis on decorating their food to make it look festive and unusual. Since help is scarce, this is not easy. This is why many of these rather fancy looking dishes, which can be made ahead of time, have been created.

Normally at a cocktail party open faced, small sandwiches are served, lavishly garnished. The two following recipes are to some extent a substitute for those time-consuming dainties. The *Striped Sandwich Loaf* can be prepared a day ahead of time and the fillings for the *Sandwich Torte* recipe also, which leaves the hostess free from last-minute preparations in the kitchen. I have suggested 4 kinds of fillings, but those can, naturally, be changed and varied.

Sweden has an enormous variety of bread, baked in many shapes. The following recipe calls for a round, white bread, I used to be able to get that from an Italian market, but if you don't have such luck, don't give up. Make instead an 8-inch square torte out of a loaf, cut in lengthwise slices, by placing 2 slices parallel for each layer. Trim edges using a ruler for a good straight edge. This will make a torte just as attractive as the round one. Instead of smoked salmon, chopped shrimp may be used in the filling. The square torte may be garnished with black caviar (or red Swedish caviar), Swedish Anchovy fillets, egg or tomato slices, olives, water cress and shrimp, see page 50.

47

Suggestions for Swedish Sandwiches

SANDWICH TORTE

1 fresh, large round white bread

Egg Cream:
6 hard-cooked eggs
1 cup butter (or cream cheese)
1–2 teaspoons curry

Salmon Cream:
1 cup cut-up smoked salmon or lax
1 cup butter (or cream cheese)
4 teaspoons tomato paste
    dash of cayenne

Garnish:
olives
lettuce
1 can Portuguese Sardines

Salmon Rolls:
2 tablespoons butter
2 tablespoons chopped dill
$1/2$ teaspoon lemon juice
4 slices Nova Scotia smoked
    salmon

Cut off top and bottom crust from bread, slice horizontally as thin as possible.

Egg Cream:

Peel eggs and chop finely. Cream butter (or cream cheese); season to taste with curry and stir in eggs.

Salmon Cream:

Chop smoked salmon or lax finely.

Cream butter (or cream cheese) with tomato paste and cayenne until soft; add salmon.

To make torte:

Spread successive layers generously with salmon and egg cream. You should have 2 layers of salmon cream and one middle of egg cream, saving remaining for the top. Press torte gently together and wrap in a damp tea towel. Keep in refrigerator for a few hours.

Before serving torte, trim edges; remove to a round serving plate.

Spread with remaining egg cream and garnish with olives, lettuce, sardines and Salmon Rolls. Serve in wedges, see color picture beside.

Salmon Rolls:

Mix butter, dill and lemon juice until soft, spread over smoked salmon slices. Roll together and wrap in waxed paper; chill.

Cut into slices.

STRIPED SANDWICH LOAF

For cocktail parties this is a perfect thing to serve. It is all made ahead of time and fillings can be varied to suit different tastes.

Cheese Cream:
3/4 cup crumbled blue cheese
3/4 cup butter or margarine
4–5 drops green food coloring

Radish Cream:

1 cup butter (half margarine)	1 loaf unsliced, white bread
1 cup finely chopped radishes	1 package pumpernickel or whole-
1 teaspoon salt	grain rye bread

Make cheese cream by mixing all ingredients until of spreading consistency. Make radish cream the same way.

Cut off top and bottom crust from white bread, slice lengthwise (or ask bakery to do so).

Place one slice of white bread on damp towel, spread generously with radish cream, cover with pumpernickel slices, placed close together, spread generously with cheese cream. Continue until radish cream is used up and there is enough cheese cream to spread over top layer, set this aside.

Wrap loaf tightly into towel and press gently between 2 boards or books. Keep in refrigerator over night.

Before serving trim edges to make even shape, spread remaining cheese cream over top and garnish with chopped radishes.

Slice loaf in rather thick slices and cut these into pieces, see color picture opposite page 46.

Keep left-over loaf in damp towel in refrigerator.

Different garnishes for Sandwich Tortes

Olika sätt att garnera Sandwichtårtor

Traditional Christmas Dishes

To Swedes, with their extremely deep feeling for tradition, Christmas has a very special meaning. Just the word Christmas calls up memories of deep snow, sleigh parties to the early Christmas morning service, Lucia parties with their special fragrance of saffron buns and coffee, and the divine smell of the many dishes prepared for Christmas from the beginning of December to the big day . . . Christmas Eve.

Most of us Swedes remember the old-fashioned Christmas preparations: the day of Anders, the thirtieth of November, when the "Lutfisk" was placed in its lye to soak; the day of Anna, the 9th of December, when the ham was put into its brine; the hog that was butchered and the many kinds of sausages that were made; the headcheese, *Jellied Veal* and *Liver Pâté* that were prepared. It was a tremendous lot of work, no doubt, but later it was all there, ready to be used during the many days of mid-winter celebrations.

Nowadays Christmas has become more streamlined with fewer preparations and fewer dishes. But still, for anybody Swedish-born and living in a foreign country, there will always be some dishes which remain of special meaning and which must be prepared for Christmas or it wouldn't be Christmas. So I selected some old-fashioned Christmas dishes and adapted the recipes to modern cooking methods in order to help you have a good old-fashioned Swedish Christmas.

Boiled "Lutfisk"
Kokt lutfisk

BOILED "LUTFISK" (LING)   KOKT LUTFISK

This is the traditional fish served for Christmas Eve Supper. Lutfisk can be bought around Christmas time in most Scandinavian markets.

4 pounds soaked lutfisk
   salt
4 tablespoons water

Skin and cut fish into serving pieces.

Place pieces close together in cheesecloth and sprinkle with salt; tie loosely.

Place in saucepan (not aluminium) and add water; bring very slowly to the boiling point; simmer gently 15–20 minutes. When ready, drain and remove to hot platter.

Serve with fresly ground black pepper and mustard, boiled potatoes, melted butter and White Sauce, see page 162.

Lutfisk may also be served with green peas.

Makes 4 servings.

HOME-CURED
CHRISTMAS HAM

This recipe is an old time favorite in Sweden, which you will find in our Christmas color picture opposite p. 14. This kind of ham has a more delicate flavor than the commercially cured. You can also use a cured, but not pre-cooked, ham and prepare it the same way with good results.

1 fresh ham (about 10–12 pounds)
1 cup salt
¹/₄ cup sugar
2 teaspoons saltpeter (available in drug stores)

Brine:
3 cups salt
³/₄ cup brown sugar, firmly packed
1 tablespoon saltpeter
2 teaspoons whole cloves
4 quarts boiling water

Seasonings:
2 bay leaves
¹/₂ teaspoon peppercorns
¹/₂ teaspoon allspice
1 chopped onion
1 chopped carrot

Glaze:
1 beaten egg white
1 tablespoon dry mustard
1 tablespoon sugar
fine, dry bread crumbs

Garnish:
cale, parsley, cooked prunes,
apple or orange sections

Mix salt, sugar and saltpeter together, rub into ham.
Place ham in large container or crock. Let stand in cool place 2–3 days.

Brine:

Add salt, sugar, saltpeter and cloves to the boiling water. Cook for a few minutes. Cool, then pour over ham. Place a light press or weighted board over ham and let stand in cold place 2–3 weeks, turning occasionally.

Remove ham from brine. (If you have possibility of sending ham to a smokehouse for 12 hours smoking, you will have a still more delicious result.)

Wipe and place in saucepan, fat-side up: cover with cold water. Bring to the boiling point, skim surface. Add seasonings, onion and carrot. Cover and simmer *very gently* for 4 hours, turning at half time.

When ham is tender, remove from liquid, skin and wipe ham with cloth removing all loose fat. Return to stock and let stand over night in a cool place – this will ensure a deliciously juicy ham.

Glaze:

Combine egg white, mustard and sugar. Brush on ham, fat-side up, and sprinkle with bread crumbs.

Bake in moderate oven (325°) until nicely brown, about 50 minutes.

Cover ham knuckle with red and white paper frill and decorate ham, if served cold, with creamed butter, forced through fine pastry tubes. Place on large platter or wooden board for carving. Serve sliced cold as part of Smörgåsbord with Spiced Red Cabbage, see page 77, and Mashed Potatoes, see page 72; or warm with Vegetables au Gratin, see page 80, or Vegetable Soufflé, see page 28.

Makes about 20 servings.

PORK SAUSAGE   FLÄSKKORV

This typical Swedish pork sausage, you will find in our Christmas color picture opposite p. 14. Nowadays it is so popular that it is not only served at Christmas time but the whole year around. For those still interested in keeping up with the old traditional way of making sausages for Christmas the two following recipes have been added.

To save a lot of work, buy the meat and let the butcher grind it and ask your butcher to order some plastic casings instead of using the oldfashioned pork casings, which are hard to clean and often break, if you stuff the casing hard.

1 pound pork fat (without meat)	$1/2$ teaspoon ground cloves
2 pounds lean pork, ground	$1/2$ teaspoon saltpeter
1 pound lean beef, ground	5 cups boiled, cold milk or strong
1 pound potatoes, peeled	pork stock or canned,
$1/2$ cup potato flour	undiluted consommé
5 teaspoons salt	6 yards straight or round casings
1 teaspoon ginger	about 2 inches wide
$1^1/2$ teaspoons coarsely ground	
black pepper	*Curing:*
1 teaspoon coarsely ground	4 tablespoons salt
allspice	2 tablespoons sugar
	1 teaspoon saltpeter

Ask your butcher to grind half the amount of the pork fat with the lean pork and beef 3 times. Dice remaining pork fat very small.

Cook potatoes 12 minutes or until half done. Pour off water and shake

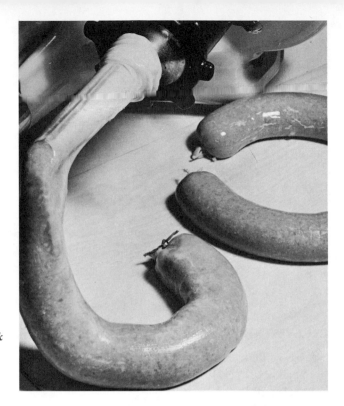

Preparing Pork Sausage

Beredning av fläskkorv

pan over heat to dry them; cool over night and mash thoroughly or put through a meatgrinder.

Place all ingredients, except the liquid, in a large bowl.

Work with your hand, while slowly adding liquid until the mixture has the consistency of a porous, but fairly thick porridge (takes about 50 minutes).

Check seasoning, if you wish, by boiling a small amount in lightly salted water for 25–30 minutes.

Order the casings ahead of time. For this kind of sausage, use fairly narrow round or straight casings. Clean casings well and cut into desired lengths. Tie each length at one end, fill loosely with a spoon or a horn attached to a meatgrinder, see picture above. Tie ends.

Rinse sausages under cold running water and drain on towel.

Combine ingredients for curing and rub on sausages, store in a large bowl in cold place.

This kind of sausage is best when eaten within a few days. If it has to be kept longer, place in cold brine. For recipe, see page 53, under Home-cured Christmas Ham.

Makes about 8 sausages.

FRIED SAUSAGE

BRÄCKKORV

The same mixture can be used for the popular Swedish sausage, named "Bräckkorv". But in that case, I would recommend using milk as liquid. Since the flavor gets stronger through the smoking procedure, cut down salt to 1 tablespoon and pepper to 1 teaspoon.

Stuff sausages rather hard.

Rinse under cold water, dry on towel and rub sausages with curing ingredients.

Smoke sausages in warm smoke for half a day.

Store, hanging in cold place.

Cut into thick slices and fry quickly. Serve with fried potatoes and scramble eggs on the Smörgåsbord or as a luncheon dish.

BOILED PORK SAUSAGE

KOKT FLÄSKKORV

2 pounds Pork Sausage, see recipe, page 54
1 bay leaf
10 peppercorns or allspice
1/2 teaspoon salt

Place sausage in large saucepan, and cover with cold water.

Add spices and salt.

Heat slowly; just before the boiling point is reached, reduce heat, cover and simmer 30 minutes.

Remove to board, cut into thick slices and place in deep serving dish with part of its liquid, see color picture opposite page 8.

Serve with Mashed Potatoes, see page 72, or Mashed Turnips, see page 79, and mustard.

SMOKED CHRISTMAS SAUSAGE   RÖKT JULKORV

*An old Swedish tradition is to make your own Smoked Christmas Sausage –
usually from a recipe handed down for generations within the same family
which is the case with this delicious recipe.*

*This kind of sausage keeps for months hanging in a cold, dry place and its
flavor improves by age. I like it best after 1–2 months, at that time the
flavor has mellowed and is wonderful! It is much cherished, thinly sliced on
sandwiches or on crackers as an appetizer.*

$2^1/_2$ pounds beef, top of round

$2^1/_2$ pounds lean pork

$2^1/_2$ pounds pork fat (without meat)

$2^1/_2$ pounds peeled potatoes

2 tablespoons salt

1 teaspoon saltpeter

2 teaspoons coarsely ground, black
   peppercorns

1 quart boiled, cold milk

$1/_3$ cup brandy

4 yards straight casings about
   3 inches wide

Curing:

3 tablespoons salt

1 tablespoon sugar

$1^1/_2$ teaspoons saltpeter

Ask the butcher to grind the beef 3 times, the last 2 times together with
the lean pork.

Ask also if he has a machine to cut the pork fat into very small dice,
otherwise get it sliced thickly and cut it criss-cross into small cubes.

Boil potatoes 12 minutes or until half cooked, pour off water and cool
over night. Put the cool potatoes through a meatgrinder.

Place all ingredients in a large bowl, except the liquids.

Work with your hand, while slowly adding liquid for one hour, or until
mixture has a porous, but firm consistency.

Order the casings ahead of time.

Clean casings very well and cut into desired lengths. Tie one end securely.

Stuff the mixture into casing by means of a horn or a sausage filler attached
to a meatgrinder, see picture, page 55. This kind of sausage must be stuffed
as hard as possible. If you get air bubbles stick with a pin and press out the
air. Tie sausages at other end, when stuffed.

Rinse sausages under cold running water, drain on towel.

Combine ingredients for curing and rub on the sausages.

Send sausages immediately to be smoked in cold smoke for 6 days.

Store sausages; if hung in dry place or stored in refrigerator they will
keep for many months.

Makes about 8 medium size sausages.

SWEDISH LIVER PÂTÉ

LEVERPASTEJ

This recipe is a real delicacy . . . The pâté is regarded by many as the best of all the cold cuts on the Smörgåsbord. In Sweden you will most likely buy it ready-made for everyday use but for Christmas almost all homemakers take a pride in making their own pâté.

In our color picture of the Swedish Christmas Smörgåsbord opposite p. 14, you will find the pâté in its oldfashioned Swedish shape, with an outer layer of pork fat.

However, I have worked out this recipe to suit a more modern taste, which has less fat and is easier to prepare.

Everybody who has traveled through Europe, I am sure, has eaten "Pâté Maison" in one or another shape as an hors d'œuvres. For those who do not intend to make a Smörgåsbord, I would recommend serving this pâté that way. It makes a very sophisticated looking appetizer. Place a $^1/_2$-inch thick slice of liver pâté on a lettuce leaf, as individual servings; garnish with tomatoes, olives or dill pickles. Serve with buttered toast.

The liver pâté can be made several days ahead of time.

1 pound calf's or beef liver	2 teaspoons salt
$^1/_2$ pound fresh pork fat, ground	$^1/_2$ teaspoon pepper, freshly ground
$^1/_2$ cup sliced onion	$^1/_4$ teaspoon ginger
3 drained Swedish Anchovy fillets	$^1/_2$ teaspoon marjoram leaves
3 eggs	3 tablespoons dry vermouth
$^2/_3$ cup light or heavy cream	1 4-ounce can mushroom buttons
3 tablespoons all-purpose flour	

There are two ways of making this dish: to put it through a meat grinder or in an electric blender, but the basic preparations remain the same.

Wash liver and dry well. If you use beef liver, soak it in milk several hours, or overnight.

Remove with sharp, pointed knife all the membrane and tubes.

For easier grinding process:

Cut liver into *small* cubes and ask your butcher to grind pork fat.

Meat grinder method:

Put liver, fat, onion and anchovies through grinder 4-5 times, using medium knife.

Add eggs one at a time, to ground mixture, beating well after each addition.

58

Gradually stir in cream, flour, seasonings, dry vermouth and sliced mushrooms, blend well.

Electric Blender method:
The container cannot do a thorough job of mincing if you load it too full. Therefore make it in three lots. Have flour and spices mixed on a piece of waxed paper and have a large mixing bowl handy.

Put into container each time about one third of ingredients, except vermouth and mushrooms. Turn off motor and scrape down several times. Let mixture blend until liver is completely puréed.

When everything is ready, and poured into the large mixing bowl, add vermouth and drained, sliced mushrooms, stir briskly until well mixed.

Butter a $9^1/_2 \times 5^1/_4 \times 2^3/_4$ inch loaf pan; spoon in liver mixture.

Cover with buttered waxed paper or aluminium foil, tie with string.

Bake in a pan filled with hot water in a slow oven (325°), for $1^3/_4$ hour, or until a thin knife inserted in the middle comes out clean.

Cool in loaf pan over night.

Invert on platter, slice and garnish with greens, dill pickles, tomatoes or red beets.

Liver Pâté keeps well if stored in refrigerator.

Makes 12–15 servings.

JELLIED VEAL KALVSYLTA

In some parts of Sweden Jellied Veal is served frequently, in other areas only at Christmas, as one of the many traditional dishes on the Christmas Smörgåsbord. It is usually accompanied with pickled red beets or Pickled Fresh Cucumber. But served as a main course with fried potatoes and a salad it is also a fine dish, especially for hot days.

This recipe has been passed on for generations within my mother's family and is one of the best kinds of Jellied Veal I ever tasted.

$2^1/_2$ pounds breast of veal with bone (the first cut is the best)	$2^1/_2$ bay leaves
1 pair of pigs knuckles about $1^1/_2$ pounds	1 large onion
	1 carrot
2 quarts cold water	2 sprigs parsley
1 tablespoon salt	2 tablespoons white vinegar
$3/_4$ teaspoon allspice	$1/_4$ teaspoon pepper, preferably
$1/_2$ teaspoon peppercorns	freshly ground

Jellied Veal made from chopped or ground meat
Kalvsylta, mald eller hackad

Place meats in large saucepan, add water and bring to the boiling point. Skim surface with spoon until clear; add salt, allspice, peppercorns, bay leaves, peeled onion, carrot and parsley. Cover and simmer $1^1/_2$ hours or until tender.

Remove meat from stock and let stand until cooled. Cut meat from bones, return bones and rinds to stock and simmer for 30 minutes.

Cut meat in the meantime into small cubes or put through grinder (should make about 5 cups loosely packed meat).

Strain stock (should measure about 7 cups). Return stock and ground meat to saucepan, add vinegar and pepper and bring to the boiling point; cook for 15 minutes, uncovered. Makes about 8 cups of liquid. Pour into molds rinsed with cold water, 2 small loaf pans or fancy shaped molds. Chill until set. Unmold for serving.

See picture above.

Makes 10–12 servings.

60

SWEDISH CHRISTMAS PORRIDGE RISGRYNSGRÖT

This is a traditional dessert for Christmas Eve

1 cup rice	1/2 cup cream
2 tablespoons butter or margarine	1 teaspoon salt
1 cup water	2 tablespoons sugar
4 cups milk	1 teaspoon vanilla
1/2 stick cinnamon	

Put rice in sieve and rinse under running cold water.

Melt half of butter or margarine in a deep saucepan; add rice and water and boil about 10 minutes, or until water disappears.

Stir in milk and cinnamon stick; cook slowly 40 minutes or until rice is tender, stirring occasionally.

Blend in cream, salt, sugar, vanilla and remaining butter or margarine.

For the real Swedish touch, add one blanched almond to porridge before pouring into hot serving dish. The one who gets the almond is supposed to get married before next Christmas.

Serve porridge with milk, sugar and cinnamon.

Makes 6 servings.

CHRISTMAS WINE JULGLÖGG

There are many ways of preparing this favorite Swedish Christmas drink, but I have found this one the most easy and the most popular among my American friends.

1 bottle Swedish aquavit or vodka	1 tablespoon cardamon seeds
2 bottles burgundy	1/2 teaspoon whole cloves
3/4 cup raisins	3 1/2-inch pieces cinnamon stick
1/2 cup sugar	1 small piece lemon peel

Pour ½ of aquavit or vodka and all of burgundy into large saucepan. Add raisins and sugar. Tie spices in cheesecloth and drop into wine mixture.

Cover pan, bring *very slowly* to the boiling point, let simmer 30 minutes. Add remaining part of gin or aquavit. Remove from heat and put a match to "glögg" in saucepan. Using a long-handled ladle, pour hot into punch glasses, see color picture opposite page 14. Serve with raisins and almonds.

To serve more effectively, before lighting pour "glögg" into a chafing dish (a good way of keeping "glögg" hot for second serving) and turn off the lights before igniting "glögg".

61

Soups

SWEDISH PEA SOUP WITH PORK

ÄRTER MED FLÄSK

Swedish Pea Soup is regarded as a real national dish. It has been served every Thursday in most Swedish homes for hundreds of years.

During the cold winter it makes a very satisfying meal, economical as well as filling. The soup is served as a main course with boiled pork. The traditional dessert after pea soup is Swedish Pancakes or "Plättar", served with jam or lingonberries, see picture beside. It makes very good eating, although it is a bit on the heavy side for modern people. If you wish a lighter dessert try the delicious Soufflé Omelet, see recipe, page 140.

The exact cooking time of the peas is hard to say, some peas take longer than others. There is no harm in overcooking, so you can easily cook soup ahead of time. This recipe is tested with dried peas that may be bought from the Swedish Delicatessen stores.

1$^1/_2$ cups dried yellow Swedish peas
2$^1/_2$ quarts water
1 pound lightly-salted side pork or 2 pounds fresh shoulder (with bone)

2 medium onions, sliced
$^1/_2$ teaspoon ginger
1 teaspoon leaf marjoram
salt and pepper to taste

Pick over and rinse peas. Turn into saucepan. Add water and soak overnight. Do not change water.

Set covered saucepan over high heat, and bring quickly to the boiling point. Remove shells floating on top of water. Cook about 2 hours.

Add pork, onions and seasonings except salt and pepper. Cover and simmer gently until pork and peas are tender, about 1 hour. Add salt and pepper to taste.

Remove pork. Cut into slices and serve separately with mustard.

Makes 4 servings.

Swedish Pea Soup, Pork, and Pancakes with Jam
Ärter med fläsk och pannkakor med sylt

FRESH PEA SOUP

FÄRSK ÄRTSOPPA

A creamy excellent soup with a beautiful color. Can be prepared ahead of time.

2 pounds fresh peas in their pods
1 quart water
1 bay leaf
1 teaspoon salt
2 tablespoons butter or margarine

4 teaspoons all-purpose flour
2 cups seasoned chicken broth or
  2 cups water and 3 chicken
  bouillon cubes
1 cup cream

Shell peas.

Wash pods, put them into large saucepan or pressure cooker with water, bay leaf and salt. Cook for 45 minutes in covered saucepan or for 20 minutes in a pressure cooker.

Drain off juice and discard pods.

Pour juice back into pan, add peas and cook over low heat 10 minutes.

Force peas through a fine sieve or put into electric blender (see below).

Melt butter or margarine in saucepan, stir in flour and purée, add liquids. Simmer stirring until smooth. Season with more salt if necessary.

Electric Blender:

Add butter or margarine and flour to peas, turn on motor. Turn off and scrape down a few times if necessary.

Pour purée back into saucepan, add liquids and simmer 5 minutes or until smooth.

Season with more salt if necessary.

Serve soup with a sprinkling of croutons (small cubes of white bread quickly fried in butter until crisp and golden colored) or serve with a dab of horseradish flavored sour cream. Mix $^1/_2$ cup of sour cream with 1–2 teaspoons grated horseradish.

Makes 6 servings.

LUSCIOUS CREAM OF MUSHROOM SOUP

CHAMPINJONPURÉ

There are many wonderful recipes in Sweden for mushroom soups, but this one is my favorite. With the help of an electric blender, it is made in a jiffy too.

3/4 pound mushrooms	1 teaspoon salt
2 tablespoons butter or margarine	1/2 teaspoon Worcestershire sauce
2 tablespoons chopped onion	1 10 1/2-ounce can consommé
2 tablespoons all-purpose flour	1 1/4 cups milk
dash of pepper	1 cup cream

Wipe mushrooms clean with damp paper towel, or rinse quickly under cold, running water; drain.

Put butter or margarine into saucepan, add onion and mushrooms; simmer covered 5 minutes.

Remove mushrooms and chop finely or place in electric blender (see below). Spoon back into pan and blend in flour, seasonings and consommé.

Cook stirring until smooth. Add milk and cream and simmer for about 10 minutes before serving.

Electric Blender:

Place mushrooms in blender. Add flour, seasonings and 1/2 cup consommé, turn on motor. Turn off and scrape down twice. Pour purée back into pan, add remaining liquids and simmer, stirring until smooth.

Makes 4 servings.

HEARTY TOMATO SOUP

LÄTTLAGAD
TOMATSOPPA

1 tablespoon shortening	2 teaspoons salt
4 slices bacon	1/8 teaspoon pepper
1 medium onion, chopped	1 6-ounce can tomato paste
(about 3/4 cup)	4 1/2 cups water
2 sliced carrots (about 3/4 cup)	1 bouillon cube or 1 teaspoon
1 tablespoon all-purpose flour	meat extract

Melt fat in large, heavy saucepan.

Cut bacon with scissors directly into fat, add onion and carrots; cook over low heat 5 minutes.

Stir in flour, salt, pepper and tomato paste. Gradually add water and bouillon cube (or meat extract); stir until well blended.

Cook covered over low heat 30–40 minutes or until vegetables are tender.

Serve with a generous tablespoon of sour cream and sprinkled with chopped dill, parsley or chives.

Makes 4 servings.

CLEAR TOMATO SOUP

KLAR TOMATSOPPA

This soup has an unusually fresh tomato flavor. Uncooked puréed tomatoes are added just before serving the soup, which makes it extra rich in vitamins too.

2 tablespoons shortening	2 cups chicken or vegetable stock
2 medium onions, chopped	2 tablespoons butter or margarine
1 clove garlic	2 tablespoons all-purpose flour
$2^1/_2$ pounds ripe tomatoes	1 bouillon cube or 1 teaspoon
2 stalks celery	meat extract
1 teaspoon salt	2 tablespoons dry vermouth or
$1/_8$ teaspoon pepper	sherry, optional

Melt fat in large saucepan; add onions and garlic and sauté 5–7 minutes.

Wash tomatoes, put aside 2 large, ripe tomatoes and break the others into saucepan. Add celery, salt, pepper and stock; cover and cook over low heat until vegetables are tender (30–40 minutes).

Force mixture through a sieve (should measure about $3^1/_2$ cups of liquid).

Melt butter or margarine in saucepan, add flour and blend well.

Stir in tomato purée and bouillon cube (or meat extract); simmer soup a few minutes.

Force the 2 remaining tomatoes through a sieve (should measure about 1 cup purée).

Add fresh tomato purée and dry vermouth or sherry just before serving, stir until well blended.

Serve sprinkled with chopped dill, celery tops or parsley.

Makes 4–5 delicious servings.

CABBAGE SOUP
WITH VEAL MEATBALLS

VITKÅLSSOPPA
MED FRIKADELLER

1 small head of green or white cabbage (about $1^1/_2$ pounds)

$1/_4$ cup shortening

1 tablespoon dark corn syrup

$1^1/_2$ quarts hot beef stock

$1/_4$ teaspoon whole allspice

$1/_4$ teaspoon peppercorns

2 teaspoons salt

Veal Meatballs, see recipe, page 67

Trim cabbage and cut into cubes, discarding core and tough portions.
Melt shortening in heavy saucepan. Add cabbage and brown lightly. Add
corn syrup and continue to brown for a few minutes, stirring.
Add stock and seasonings.
Cover closely and simmer until cabbage is tender. The cooking time for
cabbage depends on what kind of cabbage is used. Young green cabbage
will take about 20 minutes; older white cabbage about 30–40 minutes.
Add the meatballs the last 5 minutes of cooking time.
Makes 4 hearty servings.

VEAL MEATBALLS   FRIKADELLER

1/4 pound ground veal
1/4 pound ground pork
2 tablespoons fine, dry bread crumbs
1 tablespoon minced onion
1 teaspoon salt
   dash of pepper
1/4 cup cream

Combine meats, bread crumbs, onion, salt and pepper. Gradually mix
in cream.
Shape into small balls, using about a teaspoon of the mixture for each.
Boil gently in Cabbage Soup, see page 66, about 5 minutes. Or use them
for Stuffed Onions, see page 38.

EGG-BOATS   ÄGGBÅTAR

2 hard-cooked eggs
2 tablespoons butter
1 teaspoon prepared mustard
   dash of paprika

Peel eggs, cut into halves and remove egg yolks.
Mix egg yolks with butter and mustard until smooth.
Spoon mixture back into egg white shells, sprinkle with paprika.
Place one egg boat into each soup plate.

EASY TO DO
CAULIFLOWER SOUP

LÄTTLAGAD
BLOMKÅLSSOPPA

1 medium head cauliflower
(about 2 pounds)
2 cups boiling water
1 teaspoon salt
2 cups consommé or 2 cups water
and 3 bouillon cubes

$1/2$ teaspoon salt
dash of pepper
2 tablespoons butter or margarine
2 egg yolks, beaten
$1/2$ cup cream
2 tablespoons chopped parsley

Cut off tough end of stem, remove leaves and break into flowerets.

Place flowerets in large saucepan, add boiling water and salt. Cook until very tender (12–15 minutes). Then take a wire whisk and beat vigorously until cauliflower is finely minced.

Add consommé or water and bouillon cubes, and bring soup to the boiling point.

Taste soup before adding seasonings, because of varying saltiness of bouillon cubes.

Stir in butter or margarine.

Beat together egg yolks, cream and parsley. Pour egg mixture into soup beating vigorously for a few seconds and remove from heat.

Serve immediately.

Makes 4 servings.

SWEDISH VEGETABLE SOUP

GRÖNSAKSSOPPA

A rich, flavorful soup. The vegetables may be varied in kind and quantity, but keep about the same proportions of vegetables and liquid.

2 tablespoons butter or margarine
1 cup green peas, fresh or frozen
1 cup sliced carrots
3 cups water
$2^1/2$ teaspoons salt
$1^1/2$ cups raw cauliflower divided
into small flowerets

2 tablespoons all-purpose flour
$2^1/2$ cups milk
1 teaspoon Worcestershire sauce
$1/8$ teaspoon pepper
1 egg yolk
$1/2$ cup cream
2 tablespoons chives or parsley

Melt butter or margarine in saucepan.

Sauté fresh peas and carrots in fat for 5 minutes. If peas are frozen, add them later to soup before stirring in flour.

68

Stir in water and salt, bring to the boiling point, cover and simmer for 15 minutes.

Add cauliflower and continue to cook for 8 minutes.

Dissolve flour in $1/2$ cup of milk, add to soup, carefully stirring not to mash vegetables.

Add remaining milk. Season soup with Worcestershire sauce and pepper. Simmer a few minutes.

In the meantime beat egg yolk with cream and chives in a large bowl or soup tureen. Remove soup from heat, stir into egg yolk mixture and serve immediately.

Makes 6 servings.

CREAM OF SPINACH SOUP   SPENATSOPPA

A soup much appreciated in Sweden, for its nutritive value as well as for its good flavor.

1 pound fresh spinach	1 $10^1/_2$-ounce can consommé or
$1/_2$ teaspoon salt	2 bouillon cubes
3 tablespoons butter or margarine	$2/_3$ cup cream
2 tablespoons all-purpose flour	1 teaspoon lemon juice
1 cup spinach liquid or milk	1 teaspoon salt
	$1/_2$ teaspoon sugar

Rinse spinach in water; drain.

Place in saucepan with $1/_2$ teaspoon salt; cover and simmer until tender (5–8 minutes).

Remove from pan, drain, reserving liquid (should measure about 2 cups of spinach).

Chop finely or place in electric blender (see below).

Melt butter or margarine, stir in flour, spinach liquid or milk and spinach; cook, stirring until smooth.

Dilute canned consommé with $3/_4$ cup water, or dissolve bouillon cubes in 2 cups boiling water.

Add liquids and seasonings to soup, simmer until smooth.

Electric Blender:

Place spinach in container with butter or margarine, flour and $1/_2$ cup liquid, turn on motor. Turn off and scrape down a few times if necessary. Pour back into pan, add remaining ingredients; cook, stirring until smooth.

Serve soup with Egg-Boats, see recipe, page 67.

Makes 4 servings.

SWEDISH SHRIMP BISQUE

This is a delicious soup, which even "non-fish-lovers" will like. It is different from normally served soups. It can be varied to taste.

Stock:

2 tablespoons butter or margarine	10 sprigs fresh dill
2 large onions, chopped	2 quarts water
1 clove garlic, optional	1 lemon slice
3–4 pounds fresh fish	1 bay leaf
1 carrot, cut up	10 black peppercorns
3 stalks celery, chopped	1 tablespoon salt
1 tomato, chopped	1 pound shrimp, uncooked

Melt butter or margarine in large saucepan. Add onions and garlic. Simmer gently for a few minutes.

Add fish, vegetables, dill and water. Bring to a boil and skim surface until clear.

Add lemon slice, bay leaf, peppercorns and salt. Cook gently covered for 30 minutes.

Add shrimp. Cover, cook for 5–7 minutes.

Remove shrimp; peel and add to soup later.

Simmer stock for another 30 minutes and strain.

Bisque:

2 tablespoons butter or margarine	1/4 cup chopped fresh dill or chives
3 tablespoons all-purpose flour	2 egg yolks, slightly beaten
fish stock (about 6 cups)	1/2 cup heavy cream
salt	1/4 pound mushrooms, sautéed or
1–2 bouillon cubes, optional	1 3-ounce can, optional

Melt butter or margarine; stir in flour. Gradually stir in fish stock and simmer a few minutes. Season to taste with salt. Add bouillon cubes if stock doesn't have enough flavor.

Combine dill, egg yolks and cream in soup tureen or large mixing bowl.

Chop shrimp or keep whole; add to egg-cream mixture.

Optional: Add sautéed mushrooms to stock.

Bring fish stock to the boiling point and pour into tureen, beating vigorously. Serve immediately.

Makes 8 servings.

Vegetables

CHEESE-POTATO WEDGES

OSTBAKAD POTATIS

4 large potatoes
$1/_3$ cup butter or margarine
$2/_3$ cup grated, sharp cheese
1 teaspoon paprika
$1^1/_2$ teaspoons salt
2 tablespoons fine, dry bread crumbs

Peel and cut potatoes into large wedges, arrange in a single layer in buttered baking dish.
Melt butter or margarine and pour over potatoes.
Combine the other ingredients and sprinkle over potatoes.
Bake in hot oven (425°) for 30–35 minutes, or until tender and golden brown; basting occasionally with fat in baking dish.
Makes 4 servings.

BAKED POTATOES WITH CARAWAY SEED

UGNSBAKAD POTATIS MED KUMMIN

Are especially good served with pork dishes.

4 large potatoes
2 tablespoons melted butter or margarine
1 tablespoon caraway seed
$1/_2$ teaspoon salt

Select good uniform baking potatoes.
Scrub with brush and cut off a slice lengthwise of potatoes.
Brush cut surface with melted butter or margarine, sprinkle with caraway seed and salt. Place in small baking pan.
Bake in hot oven (400°) 60 minutes or until tender.
Makes 4 servings.

CREAMED POTATOES
FROM SKÅNE
SKÅNSK POTATIS

A satisfying potato dish, which can be served with many meat courses. It can also be made from cooked potatoes, which will require less milk and shorter cooking time.

1 large onion, chopped	1 cup milk
$1/4$ cup bacon drippings or	$3/4$–1 cup cream or milk
shortening	$1^1/_2$ teaspoons salt
4 cups cubed raw potatoes	$1/8$ teaspoon pepper
(about 6 medium)	2 tablespoons chopped parsley

Sauté onion in 2 tablespoons of the fat until soft, and remove from frying pan.

Add remaining fat and potatoes; fry until golden brown.

Stir in sautéed onion and milk, cook a few minutes more to see how much liquid is absorbed before adding remaining cream or milk.

Sprinkle salt and pepper over potatoes, stir until blended and cover frying pan. Cook potatoes very slowly until soft (about 15 minutes).

Pour into serving dish and sprinkle with parsley.

Makes 4 servings.

MASHED POTATOES
POTATISMOS

4 large potatoes
2 tablespoons butter or margarine
$3/4$–1 cup boiling milk
$3/4$ teaspoon salt
$1/8$ teaspoon pepper
$1/2$ teaspoon sugar

Wash and peel potatoes. Cook in slightly salted water until soft; drain.

Mash potatoes, add butter or margarine and boiling milk gradually (amount depends on how moist potatoes are); beat until smooth. Season with salt, pepper and sugar. Serve immediately.

Makes 4 servings.

BROWNED POTATOES

BRYNT POTATIS

A very nice way of serving potatoes

6 medium size boiled potatoes
3 tablespoons butter or margarine
1/4 cup fine, dry bread crumbs
1 teaspoon salt
1/2 teaspoon sugar

Shape cooked potatoes into small balls. (Use a small melon-ball cutter, if you have one; if not, cut potatoes into large cubes and round off the edges.)

Brown butter or margarine in skillet with the bread crumbs.

Mix salt and sugar together.

Add potatoes to skillet, sprinkle with part of salt and sugar. Fry quickly, (shaking pan continuously and sprinkling potato balls with remaining seasonings as they turn) until potatoes are covered with bread crumbs and nicely brown. Serve immediately.

Makes 4 servings.

ROASTED POTATOES, SWEDISH STYLE

HASSELBACKSPOTATIS

4 large baking potatoes
1/2 cup butter or shortening, melted
1 teaspoon salt
1 teaspoon paprika
1/4 cup grated cheese

Peel potatoes and slice them thinly halfway through (leaving bottom whole), see color picture opposite page 95.

Roll potatoes in melted fat and place in casserole or around roast in roasting pan. Sprinkle with salt and paprika.

Roast potatoes in moderate oven (350°) 45 minutes basting frequently with fat in pan.

Sprinkle with cheese and continue roasting potatoes without basting 20–30 minutes or until done.

Makes 4 servings.

POTATO GRIDDLE CAKES

This is a very special Swedish dish, served often for luncheon.

2 cups grated raw potatoes (about 2 large baking potatoes)
2 tablespoons sifted all-purpose flour
1 teaspoon salt
  dash of pepper

Mix grated potatoes with flour, salt and pepper. Beat until smooth.
For frying use preferably bacon fat, if not available shortening will do.
Use about 2 teaspoons of fat for each griddle cake batch when fried in a small frying pan, 1 tablespoon when frying in griddle.
These Griddle Cakes have to be fried in good, hot fat to get crisp. Drop in about 1 tablespoon of batter for each cake (they are easier to handle when not too big). Spread out batter with knife to a thin, uneven cake. Do not try to make a perfect circle; it is the uneven edge, fried to a crisp, that makes these cakes so specially good.
Fry until golden brown on both sides, turning with spatula.
Place on hot platter and serve immediately.
Serve with Fried Pork, see page 116, or bacon and lingonberries or apple sauce. See picture beside.
Makes about 18 small Potato Griddle Cakes.

WHOLE FRIED ONIONS

8 medium onions
  salt
2 cups water
2 tablespoons butter or margarine
1 teaspoon brown sugar
$1/2$ cup onion stock

Peel onions and boil in salted water 10 minutes; drain.
Brown butter or margarine in heavy frying pan.
Add onions, sprinkle with sugar and $1/2$ teaspoon salt and brown. Add onion stock.
Cover and simmer until onions are tender about 30 minutes.
Serve as part of the Smörgåsbord or with Roast Leg of Lamb, see page 120.
Makes 4 servings.

Potato Griddle Cakes with Lingonberries
Raggmunkar eller rårakor med lingonsylt

BROWN BEANS, SWEDISH STYLE

BRUNA BÖNOR

Brown beans served with Fried Pork, see picture, page 116, is one of the most traditional Swedish dishes. It is difficult to give exact measurements for seasoning because individual tastes differ. However, this recipe will help you to make brown beans that are just right and not too sweet.

The following recipe is tested with the type of dried brown beans generally found in Swedish delicatessen stores in America.

The cooking time and the amount of water required for the beans may vary, depending upon how old the beans are and the hardness of the water.

1³/₄ cups dried brown beans
5 cups water
1¹/₂ teaspoons salt
¹/₃ cup white vinegar
¹/₂ dark corn syrup
2 tablespoons brown sugar

Wash beans. Turn into saucepan and add 5 cups water. Soak over night.

Set saucepan over high heat and bring water to the boiling point quickly. Reduce heat and cook over low heat about 1 hour.

Add seasonings and continue to cook over very low heat for another hour, or until mixture thickens and beans are tender. If it doesn't thicken enough to suit your taste, remove the cover, turn up heat and stir while cooking for 5–10 minutes more. If the beans thicken too much add ¹/₄–¹/₂ cup of water.

Makes 4 servings.

STRING BEANS AU GRATIN

GRATINERADE
HARICOTS-VERTS

1 pound string beans	2/3 cup grated Cheddar cheese
4 tomatoes	1/3 cup butter or margarine

Boil string beans in lightly salted water until tender. Drain beans.

Pile string beans into serving portions on buttered fire-proof platter or in a shallow baking dish.

Cut top slice from tomatoes. Rub tomatoes with a clove of garlic and sprinkle with salt; place in middle of platter.

Sprinkle beans and tomatoes with cheese and dot with butter or margarine.

Bake in hot oven (400°) 10 minutes or until cheese has melted.

Makes 4 servings.

SPICED RED CABBAGE   KOKT RÖDKÅL

An excellent dish with many meat courses.

3 tablespoons shortening	1 cup minced onion
6 cups shredded red cabbage	1/3 cup white vinegar
(1 medium head)	1 cup water
2 tablespoons molasses	1 teaspoon salt
2 cups apple slices	1 tablespoon red currant jelly

Melt shortening in heavy skillet. Add cabbage and molasses and cook, turning, until cabbage starts to soften.

Add remaining ingredients. Cover and simmer $1-1^1/_2$ hours, stirring occasionally.

Serve warm traditionally with Roast Goose, see page 123, and Christmas Ham, see page 53, or Pork Birds, see page 113.

Makes 6 servings.

If you want to cook this dish in a pressure cooker, follow instructions for cooking cabbage on your pressure chart, using only $^1/_3$ cup of water.

MUSHROOM-STUFFED TOMATOES   SVAMPFYLLDA TOMATER

These are usually served with the Smörgåsbord, but they are also good served with a meat course or as a light luncheon dish.

1/2 pound fresh mushrooms or	dash of pepper
2 3-ounce cans	1/3 cup cream or milk
2 tablespoons butter or margarine	8 medium firm tomatoes
1 tablespoon chopped onion	2 tablespoons grated Cheddar
1 tablespoon all-purpose flour	cheese
3/4 teaspoon salt	

Clean mushrooms and chop finely.

Melt butter or margarine; sauté mushrooms with onion for 5 minutes.

Blend in flour, salt and pepper; stir in cream, cover and simmer gently for 10 minutes, stirring occasionally.

Wash tomatoes and cut off top slice; scoop out center. Sprinkle inside with salt and pepper; fill with creamed mushrooms.

Place tomatoes in buttered, shallow casserole. Sprinkle with cheese.

Bake in moderate oven (375°) for about 15 minutes or until golden brown.

Makes 4 servings.

77

SPINACH RING

*A very decorative and unusual dish, which can be served in many ways.
As a vegetable with dinner, serve it filled with rice and a border of glazed
carrots or small baked tomatoes.*

*For a light supper or for a luncheon party, fill it with Creamed Mushrooms,
see page 21, and serve garnished with crisp bacon, poached eggs and tomato
wedges.*

1 pound fresh spinach	3 eggs, beaten
2 tablespoons all-purpose flour	1 teaspoon salt
1 tablespoon soft butter or	dash of pepper
margarine	1 cup canned consommé or milk

Rinse spinach in water.

Place in saucepan, steam until tender (5–8 minutes), drain.

Chop very *finely* or place in electric blender (see below).

Place purée in large bowl, add flour, butter or margarine and beat until
very well blended. Stir in eggs, salt, pepper and liquid.

For electric blender: Put drained spinach, flour, butter or margarine, eggs
and seasonings in container and turn on motor. Pour purée into bowl, add
liquid and blend well.

Butter well a 1¹/₄ quart ring mold.

Pour spinach mixture into mold, cover with buttered waxed paper, tie
with string. Place in oven in a pan filled with hot water.

Cook in moderate oven (375°) 25 minutes, or until a knife inserted in
the middle comes out clean.

Unmold on warm serving plate, fill and serve as described above.

Makes 5–6 servings.

CAULIFLOWER WITH
EGG TOPPING

1 large head cauliflower	2 hard-cooked eggs, diced
boiling water	2 tablespoons fine, dry bread
salt	crumbs
Topping:	3 tablespoons chopped parsley
1 cup chopped onion	1 teaspoon salt
2 tablespoons butter or margarine	dash of pepper

Cut off tough end of stem, remove leaves and soak in cold, salted water with head down for 10-15 minutes.

Drain cauliflower and leave whole or break into flowerets.

Place cauliflower, head up in large saucepan. Add boiling water and bring to the boiling point without cover. Reduce heat and simmer, covered until barely tender (flowerets 8-10 minutes, whole head 12-15 minutes).

Drain, and place in hot serving dish, sprinkle with salt. Spoon topping over and serve immediately.

Topping:

Sauté onion in butter or margarine until soft, add remaining ingredients, toss lightly until blended.

Makes 4 servings.

MASHED TURNIPS   ROTMOS

2$^1/_2$ cups cubed raw turnips
  (1 medium size turnip)
3$^1/_2$ cups cubed raw potatoes
  (about 4 medium size potatoes)
1$^1/_2$ cups pork stock or water

$^1/_3$ cup milk
1 tablespoon butter or margarine
1 teaspoon sugar
$^1/_2$ teaspoon salt

Peel turnip, carefully removing all of the layer of heavy yellow peel. Cube and measure. Cook in stock or water (if just water is used, add a little salt) for about 15 minutes.

In the meantime, peel and cube potatoes. Add to turnip, after it has cooked 15 minutes and cook slowly until tender; drain. Return to heat to dry off excess water – it only takes a couple of minutes but be sure to shake pan so vegetables won't stick.

Mash the vegetables and add milk, butter or margarine, sugar and salt; mix well.

Serve with boiled salt pork, Boiled Pork Sausage, see page 56, or any suitable meat.

Makes 4-5 servings.

VEGETABLES AU GRATIN   GRÖNSAKSGRATIN

You can prepare this decorative dish ahead of time.

2 tablespoons butter or margarine
2 tablespoons all-purpose flour
1 cup milk
1/2 cup vegetable stock
1 egg yolk
1/2 cup grated Cheddar cheese

3/4 teaspoon salt
dash of pepper
4 large firm tomatoes
1 medium head cauliflower, cooked
11/2 cups cooked peas (1 package
frozen peas)

Melt butter or margarine in saucepan; blend in flour. Gradually stir in milk and vegetable stock. Stir and cook until smooth and thickened. Remove from heat.

Beat egg yolk, stir into sauce and bring to the boiling point, stirring constantly. Remove pan from heat and season sauce with $^1/_4$ cup of cheese, salt and pepper.

Cut off top slice from tomatoes.

Drain vegetables, arrange cauliflower in center, peas and tomatoes in groups around in a shallow buttered 2 quart baking dish or on a round fire-proof platter, see picture beside. Sprinkle tomatoes with salt and pepper. Pour sauce over vegetables and sprinkle with remaining cheese.

Bake in hot oven (450°) until golden brown, about 12–15 minutes; or broil until heated and golden brown.

Serve immediately either as a luncheon dish, or with a meat course for dinner.

Makes 4 servings.

MOLDED CUCUMBER SALAD   GURKSALLAD

A colorful salad, just as good as it looks.

1 envelope unflavored gelatin	1 teaspoon salt
$^1/_4$ cup cold water	1 cup sour cream
2 tablespoons grated onions	1 cup peeled, seeded and chopped
1 tablespoon lemon juice	cucumber
$^1/_2$ teaspoon sugar	

Soften gelatin in cold water for a few minutes and dissolve over heat. Add grated onions, lemon juice, sugar and salt; cool.

Pour sour cream into mixing bowl. Beat on medium speed, gradually adding the gelatin mixture. Mix until well blended.

Drain cucumber and fold into cream mixture.

Brush a 1 quart mold with oil.

Spoon mixture into mold; chill until firm.

Invert mold on platter. Arrange lettuce and carrot sticks around; sprinkle these with lemon juice or French Dressing.

French Dressing:

Crush 1 clove of garlic and place in a jar.

Add 1 tablespoon tarragon vinegar, 2 tablespoons oil and $^1/_2$ teaspoon salt. Place the lid over the jar and shake well.

MIXED SALAD

1 head of lettuce
1 bunch radishes
2 hard-cooked eggs
4 small tomatoes
2 tablespoons chopped chives

Dressing:
3 tablespoons olive or salad oil
1 tablespoon tarragon vinegar
1/2 teaspoon prepared mustard
1/2 teaspoon salt
dash of pepper

Wash, dry and crisp lettuce. Break leaves into pieces and place in salad bowl.

Clean radishes and slice thinly.

Separate cooked egg yolks from whites and chop each coarsely.

Peel and slice tomatoes.

Arrange sliced tomatoes, chopped egg yolks, sliced radishes and chopped egg whites in rings on top of lettuce, with chopped chives in center.

Mix ingredients for dressing until well blended. Pour over salad just before serving and toss lightly.

Serve with meat or fish, or as a Smörgåsbord dish.

Makes 4 servings.

POTATO SALAD

6-8 medium size cold, boiled
  potatoes
1/4 cup chopped onions
2 tablespoons chopped parsley
2 tablespoons chopped chives or
  chopped capers
1/2 cup diced pickled beets

Dressing:
2 tablespoons vinegar
6 tablespoons salad oil
1 teaspoon salt
1/4 teaspoon pepper

Combine ingredients for dressing thoroughly; pour into salad bowl.

Slice potatoes into salad bowl, add onions and toss until blended. (Let stand a few hours or over night covered with foil in refrigerator.)

Arrange parsley, chives, and beets in rows on top before serving.

Toss ingredients once or twice just before serving.

Serve on the Smörgåsbord, or with hot dogs.

Makes 6 servings.

TOMATO SALAD

Try this for a change. I am sure you will like it and there's no need for last-minute salad preparation.

4 large, ripe tomatoes	*Dressing:*
1/2 teaspoon salt	1 tablespoon prepared mustard
dash of pepper	1 tablespoon vinegar
3 tablespoons chopped scallions	1 tablespoon sugar
2 tablespoons chopped parsley,	1/2 cup sour cream
dill or celery tops	

Peel tomatoes, slice thinly and arrange on serving platter or on individual dishes.

Sprinkle tomatoes with salt, pepper, scallions and parsley.

Mix mustard with vinegar and sugar; gradually stir in sour cream. Spoon dressing over tomatoes. (Poke lightly with fork to separate slices, so that dressing can penetrate.)

Chill salad a few hours.

Garnish with lettuce or celery tops before serving.

Makes 4 servings.

ITALIAN SALAD
ITALIENSK SALLAD

Despite its name, this is a typical Swedish salad, often found on the Smörgåsbord.

It can be served as is, lavishly garnished with greens, twisted cucumber and tomato slices, or it can be spread on slices of cold cooked ham and shaped into cornucopias or rolls. Garnished with tomato wedges and canned asparagus spears, it makes a very attractive main course for hot days.

1 cup mayonnaise	1 cup canned, extra small peas
1/2 cup heavy cream, whipped	1/4 cup finely chopped dill pickles
1 teaspoon prepared mustard	1 cup chopped, cooked spaghetti
1 cup cooked, finely chopped	11/2–2 cups finely chopped,
carrots	cooked, smoked ham, tongue or
1 cup peeled, chopped apple	luncheon meat

Blend together mayonnaise, cream and mustard; season to taste.

Stir in remaining ingredients (if salad is to be served as filling, omit meat).

Chill salad before serving.

BROILED TOMATOES

4 large tomatoes
1 clove of garlic
$1/4$ teaspoon salt
  dash of pepper

1 tablespoon soft butter or margarine
1 tablespoon chopped parsley, dill or chives

Cut off top slices from tomatoes, rub surface with garlic and sprinkle with salt and pepper.

Mix butter or margarine with chopped parsley and spread over tomatoes.

Broil 4–5 inches from heat for about 5 minutes or until tomatoes start to get soft and have a nice color.

Makes 4 servings.

APPLE SALAD

4 good, tart apples
$3/4$ cup cream

1–3 tablespoons lemon juice
1–3 teaspoons sugar

Peel, shred or grate apples coarsely.

Mix cream with lemon juice and sugar (amount depends on tartness of apples).

Pour sauce over apples, toss lightly and chill.

Serve cold, sprinkled with nuts or paprika on the Smörgåsbord or with pork dishes.

Makes 4 servings.

PICKLED FRESH CUCUMBER

2 medium size cucumbers
⅓ cup white vinegar
2 tablespoons water
$1/4$ cup sugar

$1/2$ teaspoon salt
  dash of pepper
2 tablespoons chopped parsley

Wash cucumber (do not peel) and slice thinly. Place in a deep bowl.

Mix vinegar, water, sugar, salt and pepper thoroughly. Pour over cucumber and sprinkle with parsley.

Select a plate which will rest directly on cucumber in bowl. Weight down and refrigerate about 3 hours before serving.

Serve with meat. See color picture opposite page 95.

Makes 4 servings.

Fish Dishes

Since Sweden is a peninsula, fishing is of great importance to its population. You will find many fish canning industries on the West Coast which specialize in making all the famous tidbits and anchovies without which no true Smörgåsbord could ever be served. Only by using these Swedish products will you know how Swedish dishes are really supposed to taste.

Because fish is such an important item in Sweden, you will understand why it is on Swedish menus so often. It has become popular because Swedish homemakers have special ways with fish. They use fresh dill in cooking herring and other fish dishes and serve the fish with potatoes that have been boiled with dill sprigs to bring out all the flavor. But when the fish, such as pike and salmon, has a distinctive flavor of its own they do not mask it, but season delicately to accent the natural taste. On the other hand, they can add flavor to bland-tasting fish to make it more appetizing, as in *Baked Fish Gourmet*.

The most highly regarded fish in Sweden is the fresh-caught salmon. It is a great delicacy when served poached in *Court Bouillon* with a good *Hollandaise Sauce* and tiny new potatoes. But it is also very good when lightly salted and smoked, and served with *Creamed Spinach* and poached eggs.

Many other kinds of fish, both from the lakes and the sea, are treated with skill and imagination and they all deserve to become known to other nationalities and take a place among their favorite dishes.

Preparing Stuffed Herring
Beredning av strömmingsflundror

FRIED STUFFED HERRING
OR SMELT FILLETS

**2 pounds fresh herring or
    smelts
1¹/₂ teaspoons salt
3 tablespoons butter or margarine
¹/₂ cup chopped parsley**

**1 egg, beaten
¹/₂ cup fine, dry bread crumbs
¹/₂ cup oil**

Clean fish, removing heads and tails. Rinse fish under cold running water and drain.

Split and bone fish. Leave them whole.

Spread out fish, skin-side down, and sprinkle with salt.

Cream butter or margarine with parsley and spread on half of the fish; top with remaining fish, to form sandwiches.

Dip in beaten egg, then coat with bread crumbs, see picture above.

86

Heat oil in frying pan; add fish and sauté on each side until golden brown. Remove to hot platter.

Serve with Mashed Potatoes, see page 72, and Mixed Salad, see page 82.

Makes 4 servings.

PICKLED FRIED FRESH HERRING OR SMELTS

INLAGD STEKT STRÖMMING

2 pounds fried herring or
 smelts (see recipe, page 86)
3/4 cup white vinegar
1/4 cup water

1/2 cup sugar
10 peppercorns
1 onion, sliced
dill sprigs

Fry herring or smelts as directed in recipe, see page 86; let stand until cold.

Combine remaining ingredients and mix well; pour over cold fried fish. Chill in refrigerator 2-4 hours or over night.

Serve as part of Smörgåsbord or as a luncheon dish with a salad.

Makes 4 servings.

FRIED SALT HERRING

STEKT SALT SILL

2 salt herring
 fine, dry bread crumbs or rye flour
3-4 tablespoons butter or margarine
2-3 onions, sliced
1/2 cup cream

Clean and fillet fish, removing skin; soak fillets over night in cold water. Dry with absorbent paper.

Coat with bread crumbs or flour.

Melt 1 tablespoon of butter or margarine in frying pan; add onions and sauté until tender; remove onions from pan and keep warm.

Sauté fish in remaining butter or margarine until golden brown.

Pour cream over fillets and simmer for a few minutes. Remove fillets to hot platter. Top fillets with cream and onions.

Onions and cream may be omitted and fish served with Onion Sauce, see page 166.

Serve with boiled or baked potatoes.

Makes 4 servings.

BAKED FISH GOURMET

*If your husband belongs to the large group of men who say they don't care
for fish at home, he will be converted after eating this dish.*

4 slices bacon	2 teaspoons salt
1 cup sliced carrots	$1/8$ teaspoon pepper
1 cup chopped onion	1 2-pound slice of halibut or
$1/4$ pound mushrooms, chopped	other fish suitable for baking
2 tablespoons chopped parsley	4 lemon slices
2 tablespoons sliced celery	2 tablespoons butter or margarine
$1/2$ teaspoon chopped dill or thyme	$3/4$ cup dry, white wine or chicken
	broth

Place bacon slices and chopped ingredients in bottom of a shallow baking
dish, season with 1 teaspoon salt and pepper.

Put fish on top, sprinkle with remaining salt, and arrange lemon slices
over fish; dot with butter or margarine.

Pour white wine or chicken broth over fish, cover with foil and bake in
moderate oven (375°) for 20 minutes.

Remove foil and bake 15–20 minutes longer or until fish flakes easily
when pierced with a fork.

Serve with Mashed Potatoes, see page 72, and Mixed Salad, see page 82.
Makes 4 servings.

POACHED COD, SWEDISH STYLE

KOKT TORSK

1 3-pound fresh cod	3 carrots, sliced
boiling water	2 teaspoons salt
1 large onion, halved	

The cod should be cleaned without removing the head. The liver should
be saved.

Wrap fish and liver in some cheesecloth, arrange in a pan and cover with
boiling water. Add onion, carrots and salt. Bring to the boiling point slowly,
reduce heat and simmer until the fish flakes easily when pierced with a fork.
Allow about 20–25 minutes.

Transfer fish to a hot platter. Garnish it with the carrots and the onion.

The Swedes prize the head and the liver. These as well as the flesh of the
cod are eaten with hot melted butter and freshly grated horseradish.

Makes 4 servings.

Poached Fillets with Lemon Sauce
Fiskrulader med citronsås

POACHED FILLETS WITH LEMON SAUCE

FISKRULADER MED CITRONSÅS

2 pounds fillets of flounder, cod, or haddock
1 teaspoon salt
6 sprigs fresh dill
2 cups water
2 or 3 onion slices

1 bay leaf
2 whole allspice
2 peppercorns
2 teaspoons salt
1 lemon slice
Lemon Sauce, see recipe, page 162

Cut fillets into 6 pieces. Sprinkle with 1 teaspoon salt. Place a dill sprig on each and roll up; fasten with toothpicks.

Combine remaining ingredients in skillet and simmer 10-15 minutes. Strain.

Place fillets in skillet. Pour strained liquid over fish; cover and simmer 10–15 minutes.

Remove fish to hot serving platter. Pour Lemon Sauce over fish and garnish with lemon sections and dill, see picture above.

Serve with Mashed Potatoes, see page 72. Makes 6 servings.

PIKE WITH HORSERADISH SAUCE

KOKT GÄDDA MED
PEPPARROTSSÅS

A very typical Swedish fish recipe.

2–2¹/₂ pounds pike
1 quart boiling water
1 tablespoon salt
2–3 slices onion
Horseradish Sauce, see recipe, page 162

Clean fish. Cut off fins and gills with scissors. Rinse fish well under cold running water. Drain.

Boil water with salt and onion for 5 minutes. Wrap fish in cheesecloth and add to boiling water. Cover and simmer until fish is done, about 20 minutes. Remove fish to hot serving platter and garnish with parsley and tomatoes.

Serve with Horseradish Sauce or with grated fresh horseradish and melted butter.

Leftover boiled pike makes a delicious Fish Soufflé, see page 29.

Makes 6 servings.

FISH WITH VEGETABLES

FISKRÄTT MED
GRÖNSAKER

A simple but good fish dish, which includes the vegetables.

2 tablespoons butter or margarine
2 large onions or leeks, sliced
2¹/₂ cups sliced carrots
1 cup water
1 teaspoon salt
1 slice lemon
1 slice onion
1–2 stalks celery
1¹/₂ pounds cod, haddock or
    flounder fillets

Sauce:
2 tablespoons butter or margarine
3 tablespoons all-purpose flour
1 cup fish stock
¹/₂ cup light cream or milk
1 tablespoon lemon juice
³/₄ teaspoon salt

Fish with Vegetables served with Mashed Potatoes
Fiskrätt med grönsaker och potatismos

Melt 1 tablespoon butter or margarine in frying pan, add onions or leeks, cover and sauté in butter until soft. Prepare carrots the same way.

Combine water, salt, lemon, onion and celery in wide, shallow pan. Bring slowly to the boiling point. Add fish fillets and simmer until fish flakes easily when pierced with a fork (about 8 minutes).

Drain fish when done; arrange on heated platter, keep warm.

Sauce:

Melt butter or margarine, add flour. Gradually stir in strained fish stock and cream, season with lemon juice and salt.

Pour sauce over fish and garnish with rows of the vegetables on top. See picture above.

Makes 4 servings.

Ingredients for Marinated Salmon   Ingredienser till gravad lax

Marinated Salmon with Dressing   Gravad lax med dressing

MARINATED SALMON

This dish is regarded as a great delicacy in Sweden and is very popular during summer time when there is plenty of dill and fresh-caught salmon. If you can't get dill, don't try this dish.

3 tablespoons salt (preferably
   coarse salt)
3 tablespoons sugar
1 teaspoon black peppercorns,
   crushed
2 large bunches fresh dill

Dressing:
  3 tablespoons olive or salad oil
  2 teaspoons vinegar
  $1^1/_2$ teaspoons prepared mustard
  $1/_4$ teaspoon salt
    dash of pepper
    dash of sugar

Select middle cut of salmon. Clean fish and rinse under cold running water. Dry with absorbent paper. Cut fish along the back; carefully remove bone.

Mix together salt, sugar and crushed peppercorns. Rub part of seasonings into fish, see pictures beside.

Place a thick layer of dill sprigs in bottom of pan or large bowl. Set one piece of salmon, skin side down, on dill; sprinkle with seasonings and plenty of dill sprigs. Set other piece of salmon, skin side up, over salmon in pan; sprinkle with remaining seasonings and dill.

Set board on top of fish and weight down. Refrigerate at least 24 hours, preferably 3-4 days.

Scrape off spices and cut salmon into thick slices. Arrange on serving platter and garnish with fresh dill and lemon wedges.

Combine ingredients for dressing and serve with salmon.

Marinated Salmon may be served as a main dish or as an appetizer with the Smörgåsbord. It will keep for some time in the refrigerator but will be more salty if kept long.

Makes 8 servings.

POACHED SALMON IN ASPIC

KOKT LAX I GELÉ

This is so pretty, easy to prepare and to serve.

Cook fish as in Poached Salmon, see recipe, page 94; when cold, remove skin and place on serving platter. Garnish with cucumber slices.

Strain bouillon through double layers of cheese cloth, add 1 envelope unflavored gelatin to each pint of cold liquid. Heat until gelatin is dissolved.

Cool until consistency of syrup. Spoon half amount over fish, place fish in refrigerator for 15 minutes and spoon remaining gelatin mixture over fish. Garnish salmon with tomatoes filled with Pickled Fresh Cucumber, see page 84, and mayonnaise. See color picture of Smörgåsbord between pages 14 and 15.

POACHED SALMON   KOKT LAX

2 pounds salmon
Court Bouillon, see recipe below
   dill sprigs or parsley
   lemon slices

Rinse and clean fish; wrap in cheese cloth and tie the ends so that it will be easy to lift out of the pan.

Bring Court Bouillon to a gentle boil. Lower salmon into simmering liquid. Simmer covered for 20–25 minutes. Do not overcook, flesh should be flaky and firm, not mushy.

Carefully remove fish from bouillon. Arrange on serving dish and garnish with dill or parsley sprigs, and lemon slices.

Serve hot with Hollandaise Sauce, see page 165.

Makes 6 servings.

Fish may also be served cold as part of Smörgåsbord. Prepare as above, but after the fish has been removed from the bouillon, strain the bouillon, return the fish to it and chill.

Serve with grated fresh horseradish and sour cream, or with mayonnaise. Garnish platter with tomatoes and cucumbers.

You may use trout, mackerel or eel instead of salmon, but these fishes will cook in about 15–20 minutes.

Court Boullion

1 quart water	**1 bay leaf**
3 tablespoons white vinegar	**1 small onion, chopped**
1 tablespoon salt	**1 small carrot, chopped**
5 whole allspice	**4–5 sprigs dill or parsley**

Combine all ingredients in skillet or saucepan. Bring to the boiling point; cover and simmer 15 minutes.

Use as stock; see Poached Salmon above.

94

BOILED LOBSTER

4 quarts water
$1/2$ cup salt
5-10 sprigs or crowns of fresh dill
1 lobster

Bring water, salt and dill to the boiling point. Cook 2 minutes.
Plunge live lobster, head first, into vigorously boiling water. Cover and simmer 18 minutes for 2-pound lobster, 15 minutes for 1-pound, 12 minutes for $1/2$-pound. Allow to cool in stock.
Split lobster and crack claws with a nutcracker; remove dark intestinal vein and stomach.
Arrange lobster on platter and garnish with dill and lemon slices. Serve with mayonnaise or with Dressing as given for Marinated Salmon, see page 93, and toast and butter.
A 1-pound lobster gives about 1 cup of cubed lobster meat.

CRAYFISH

The beginning of the Swedish crayfish season in August is celebrated with special parties, see color picture opposite page 94. Crayfish are regarded as a great delicacy.

40 crayfish
4 quarts of water
5 tablespoons salt
  plenty of dill crowns

Crayfish must be alive before boiling.
Wash thoroughly in cold water.
Boil water, salt and dill 2–3 minutes; remove dill.
Plunge crayfish into rapidly-boiling water – add 10 or 15 fish first, then again bring water to a rapid boil before adding remaining fish.
Cover and boil gently 6–7 minutes.
Add more dill and allow crayfish to cool in the stock; chill before serving.
Arrange on platter and garnish with crowns of dill.
Makes 4 servings.

Veal Roast with Roasted Potatoes, Swedish Style. Pickled
Fresh Cucumbers and Vegetables. Lemon Chiffon Pudding

Preparing Stuffed Fish
Beredning av Hel fisk i kapprock

STUFFED FISH   HEL FISK I KAPPROCK

This is a delicate fish dish, which is best served during the summer because it requires plenty of fresh herbs such as dill, parsley and chives. None of the flavors are lost during cooking since the fish is baked wrapped in waxed paper.

**4 small mackerel or 2 large
mackerel or 4 trout
2 teaspoons salt
2 teaspoons lemon juice**

Stuffing:
**$1/4$ cup butter or margarine
$1/4$ cup chopped dill
$1/4$ cup chopped parsley
$1/4$ cup chopped chives
2 tablespoons chopped green onion
2 tablespoons lemon juice**

Wash fish under cold running water; drain on absorbent paper. Rub inside and out with salt and lemon juice.

Stuffing:

Soften butter or margarine. Add balance of ingredients, one at a time, blending thoroughly before adding the next. Pack stuffing into fish.

96

Tear off sheets of waxed paper about $1^1/_2$ times as large as the fish. Place fish in the middle of each. Fold paper drugstore-style over fish so it is well sealed in the paper, see picture, page 96. Place packages in baking dish. Bake in hot oven (400°) 15 10 minutes for large mackerel, 10-12 for trout and small mackerel.

Serve immediately, with Mashed Potatoes, see page 72.

Makes 4 servings.

BAKED EEL UGNSTEKT ÅL

1 eel (about 2 pounds)	3 tablespoons fine, dry bread
$1^1/_2$ teaspoons salt	crumbs
juice of half lemon	1 teaspoon salt
1 egg, beaten	2 tablespoons butter or margarine

Loosen skin around neck of eel and draw off skin with piece of cloth held in hand.

Remove head, split eel open and clean thoroughly. Remove backbone, being careful not to pierce meat.

Rub with the $1^1/_2$ teaspoons salt and lemon juice; brush with egg.

Mix bread crumbs and salt; sprinkle over eel. Place in well buttered baking dish.

Dot with butter or margarine.

Bake in hot oven (400°) about 40 minutes for whole eel or 25 minutes if cut into small pieces – baste frequently and add a little hot water if needed.

Serve hot or cold, with boiled potatoes, Mixed Salad, see page 82, and Sharp Sauce, see page 163.

Makes 4 servings.

SOUR SMELTS SURSTRÖMMING

If you are from the North of Sweden, you will probably be absolutely "mad" about this dish, which is traditional for that part of Sweden.

Canned Sour Smelts may be served directly from can or arranged on serving dish. If served from can, open $^1/_2$ hour before serving time, to allow odor to disappear; tie a napkin around can. If arranged on serving dish, rinse smelts in sodawater, drain and keep in cool place until serving time.

Serve with finely-chopped onion, boiled new potatoes, thin hard bread. "Tunnbröd", butter and Swedish or Norwegian goat cheese.

FISH AU GRATIN

This is a wonderful dish for entertaining. Since it includes potatoes, a vegetable salad is all you need to round out the main course. Fish au Gratin can be completely prepared ahead of time and placed in the oven just before serving.

2 pounds fillets of sole or flounder, fresh or frozen
2 teaspoons salt
3 tablespoons lemon juice
2 tablespoons butter or margarine
$1/2$ pound mushrooms

Sauce:
1 tablespoon butter or margarine
2 tablespoons all-purpose flour
1 cup fish stock

2 egg yolks
$1/3$ cup heavy cream
$1/3$ cup cold butter
$1/2$ teaspoon salt

Topping:
Duchesse Potatoes (recipe follows)
$1/2$ cup grated Cheddar cheese
1 tablespoon melted butter or margarine

Rinse fillets under cold running water. Dry with absorbent paper. Sprinkle with salt. Place in buttered shallow baking dish; sprinkle with lemon juice and dot with 1 tablespoon butter or margarine. Cover dish with buttered waxed paper. Bake in hot oven (425°) for 10 minutes.

Let fish cool in stock. Drain fish, reserving stock for sauce, measure and add water if necessary to make 1 cup.

Arrange fish in buttered shallow baking dish, or on buttered fireproof serving plate.

Sauté mushrooms 5 minutes in remaining tablespoon butter or margarine and chop finely or place in electric blender with its juice.

Sauce:

Melt 1 tablespoon butter in saucepan. Remove from heat and stir in flour. Gradually stir in stock. Cook, stirring constantly until smooth and thick. Remove from heat.

Beat egg yolks with cream; stir into sauce. Return to heat and bring to the boiling point, stirring constantly. Remove pan from heat and gradually add cold butter and salt, stirring constantly. Blend in mushrooms with their juice.

Spread sauce over fish.

Topping:

Force Duchesse Potatoes (see following recipe) through pastry tube around edge of baking dish or drop by the spoonful; brush with melted butter or margarine, see picture beside.

Preparing Fish au Gratin
Beredning av fiskgratin

Sprinkle cheese over potatoes and fish.

Brown in a broiler 5 inches from heat or in a hot oven (450°) about 8–10 minutes or until golden brown.

If you have prepared this dish ahead of time and have had it in a refrigerator for several hours the cooking time will be slightly longer.

Makes 6 servings.

Duchesse Potatoes   POTATISMOS

4 large potatoes (or 1 quart	2 egg yolks
mashed potatoes)	1 teaspoon salt
1 tablespoon butter or margarine	$1/2$ teaspoon sugar
$1/4$ cup milk or cream	dash of pepper

Peel potatoes and boil in salted water until tender; drain.

Put through potato ricer, or mash thoroughly.

Add butter or margarine, milk or cream, egg yolks and seasonings; beat well.

Press mounds onto buttered baking sheet and broil, or bake in hot oven (450°), until golden; or force through pastry tube as in recipe for Fish au Gratin.

Fried Halibut Steaks with Capers and Lemon
Stekt hälleflundra med kapris och citron

FRIED HALIBUT STEAKS WITH CAPERS AND LEMON

STEKT HÄLLEFLUNDRA
MED KAPRIS OCH CITRON

This recipe does wonders for frozen as well as fresh fish and it is easy to prepare.

2 large halibut steaks, $3/4$–1 inch thick
$1/2$ cup fine, dry bread crumbs
$1^1/2$ teaspoons salt

$1/2$ cup butter or margarine
$1/4$ cup capers
1 lemon

Cut steaks into 4 pieces.

Coat fish with bread crumbs, mixed with salt.

Melt butter or margarine in large frying pan. Brown fish slowly on each side, until golden yellow.

Place on hot serving platter.

Sprinkle with capers and garnish with lemon slices or sections, see picture above.

Serve immediately, with additional melted butter, Mashed Potatoes, see page 72, and Tomato Salad, see page 83. Makes 4 servings.

100

Meat Dishes

There are many very simple meat dishes that represent cooking at its best to the Swedish taste, but these same dishes may not seem so special to people of other countries at first. This is the case with national dishes of many of the countries I have made acquaintance with, yet they are worth trying. However, it is understandable that we have a weakness for our own national dishes, since our tastes are formed in youth. Because it is hoped that this book will provide up-to-date recipes for people other than Swedes, as well as for the Swedish, I have included such old specialties as *Fried Pork with Brown Beans, Swedish Beefsteak with Onions, Stuffed Cabbage Leaves, Swedish Meatballs*, to mention a few; but also many dishes of the modern Swedish cuisine such as *Braised Beef Rolls, Pork Chops Piquant* and *Gourmet Lamb.*

The Swedish homemaker is very thrifty and uses up every little scrap of a roast. So good gravies and sauces play an important part in her cooking, especially when she is using a cheaper cut of meat, for instance the *Royal Pot Roast.* One of the most delightful Swedish dishes is made just from left-overs, *Swedish Hash* or *"Pytt i Panna"*, a delicacy when made with care and good seasoning.

But each dish has its special flavoring and its special little touch which is what makes Swedish cooking interesting for the homemaker to explore and a joy for the family to eat.

SWEDISH BEEFSTEAK WITH ONIONS   BIFF MED LÖK

A rich flavorful dish with a special "man" appeal.

2 pounds sirloin steak
$1/4$ cup butter or margarine
4 onions, sliced
1 teaspoon salt
$1/4$ teaspoon pepper
$1/2$ cup boiling water

Cut steak into 4 serving portions. Pound meat lightly with meat hammer or edge of heavy saucer.

Melt 2 tablespoons of the fat in skillet. Add onions and sauté until tender and nicely brown. Remove onions from pan and keep warm.

Add remaining butter or margarine to pan; heat.

Sprinkle meat with salt and pepper. Fry in butter or margarine 3–4 minutes on each side, or longer if desired.

Remove meat to hot serving platter. Pour boiling water into skillet and stir to dissolve brown particles in pan; pour over meat. Garnish steaks with onions, see picture beside.

Serve immediately with fried potatoes.

Makes 4 servings.

BOILED BEEF WITH HORSERADISH SAUCE

KOKT NÖTKÖTT MED PEPPARROTSSÅS

3 pounds brisket of beef (first cut preferably) or 3 pounds chuck
1 quart boiling water
1 tablespoon salt
1 carrot, cut up
3 stalks celery, chopped

4 sprigs parsley
1 onion, chopped
$1/4$ teaspoon black peppercorns
5 whole allspice
1 bay leaf
Horseradish Sauce, see page 163

Place meat in saucepan and add boiling water. Bring to the boiling point and remove scum from surface until clear.

Add salt, vegetables and spices, and bring water to the boiling point. Cover and simmer about 2 hours, or until meat is tender.

Slice meat. Arrange on hot serving platter. Serve with boiled potatoes, vegetables and Horseradish Sauce.

Makes 5–6 servings.

Swedish Beefsteak with Onions
Biff med lök

SAILORS' BEEF

SJÖMANSBIFF

A good hearty dish for cold days.

1¹/₂ pounds chuck or round of beef
5–6 medium potatoes
2 tablespoons butter or margarine
2 cups sliced onions
2 teaspoons salt
   dash of pepper

³/₄ cup water
³/₄ cup beer
   chopped parsley

103

Cut meat into $^1/_2$-inch thick slices. Pound a little with meat hammer or edge of heavy saucer.

Peel potatoes and cut into $^1/_2$-inch thick slices (about 4 cups potato slices).

Heat butter or margarine in skillet. Add meat and brown quickly on both sides; sprinkle with 1 teaspoon of the salt. Remove meat from skillet.

Cook onions in the same skillet until brown. Remove from pan.

Add water to pan and cook a few minutes.

Place meat, onions and potatoes in alternate layers in a 2 quart casserole, sprinkling each layer with remaining salt and pepper. Add pan liquid and beer.

Cover and bake in moderate oven (375°) 1–1$^1/_4$ hours, or until meat is tender.

Sprinkle with chopped parsley before serving.

Makes 4 servings.

BEEF STEW   KALOPS

This stew is a favorite with many Swedish men. Is best when prepared ahead of time since the flavor improves when the dish is reheated.

2$^1/_2$ pounds beef chuck (with a few   4 medium onions, preferably red
   bones left in for the flavor)   onions

2 teaspoons salt $^1/_2$ teaspoon whole allspice

$^1/_4$ teaspoon pepper   2 bay leaves

3 tablespoons all-purpose flour   1$^1/_2$ cups boiling water

2 tablespoons butter or margarine

Cut meat across the fibres into large cubes.

Combine salt, pepper and flour in a paper bag. Add meat and shake until pieces are evenly coated.

Heat butter or margarine in a heavy skillet or saucepan. Add meat and brown well.

Peel onions and cut each into 6 sections. Add to meat with spices and boiling water. Cover and let simmer over low heat until meat is tender, about 1 – 1$^1/_2$ hours.

Remove meat to deep serving dish. Strain pan liquid and pour over meat. Serve with boiled potatoes, vegetables and pickled beets, or lingonberries.

Makes 6 servings.

*Preparing Beef
Rolls*

Beredning av
oxrulader

BRAISED BEEF ROLLS

OXRULADER

A good dish to prepare ahead of time; popular with both old and young.

2 pounds round beef, $1/4$-inch thick
$3/4$ teaspoon salt
$1/4$ teaspoon pepper
2 teaspoons prepared mustard
8 slices bacon
4 hot dogs

2 tablespoons all-purpose flour
2 tablespoons butter or margarine
1 bouillon cube
$1/2$ cup boiling water
$1/4$ cup cream or milk

105

Ask your butcher to pound the meat thin and flat.

Cut beef into 8 strips about $4 \times 2^{1}/_{2}$ inches.

Sprinkle meat on both sides with salt and pepper. Spread one side with mustard. Place one slice of bacon and half a hot dog on mustard side of each piece of meat, see picture, page 105; roll up and secure with toothpicks or string. Coat with flour.

Heat butter or margarine in heavy skillet. Add meat and brown well on all sides.

Dissolve bouillon cube in boiling water and pour into skillet. Cover tightly and simmer until meat is tender, about 1 hour. Lift beef rolls from pan. Remove string or toothpicks and place rolls in hot, deep serving dish and keep warm.

Add cream or milk to gravy in pan. Bring to the boiling point, stirring constantly. Pour over beef rolls.

Serve with Browned Potatoes, see page 73, String Beans au Gratin, see page 76, and lingonberries.

Makes 4 servings.

ROYAL POT ROAST   SLOTTSSTEK

This variation of Pot Roast has a wonderful flavor.

4 pounds round or rump of beef	2 tablespoons white vinegar or cider
2 teaspoons salt	2 tablespoons brandy or
$1/2$ teaspoon pepper	dry vermouth, optional
2 tablespoons butter or margarine	2 tablespoons molasses
½ cup bouillon or water	*Gravy:*
2 onions, sliced	2 cups pan drippings
3 Swedish anchovy fillets or	3 tablespoons all-purpose flour
½ teaspoon anchovy paste	$1/4$ cup water
2 bay leaves	1 cup cream
$1/2$ teaspoon whole allspice	1 tablespoon anchovy juice or
$1/4$ teaspoon peppercorns	$1/4$ teaspoon anchovy paste

Rub meat with salt and pepper.

Heat butter or margarine in Dutch oven or heavy kettle. Add meat and brown well on all sides. Add bouillon (1 bouillon cube dissolved in 1 cup boiling water) and all remaining ingredients. Cover closely and simmer gently until meat is tender, about 2 hours. Remove meat to hot serving platter and keep warm.

106

Gravy:

Strain pan drippings and measure and return to the pan. Blend flour and water; pour into drippings, Cook, stirring, over low heat until smooth and thick. Stir in cream and cook for about 5 minutes more. Remove from heat and stir in anchovy juice or anchovy paste.

Slice meat and serve with the gravy and suitable vegetables.

Makes 6–8 servings.

VEAL ROAST   KALVSTEK

A roast very often served in Sweden especially on Sundays. Cooked this way, the veal will be very juicy and the gravy delicious.

4¹/₂–5 pounds rump of veal	**2 onions, sliced**
(with bone)	**¹/₂ teaspoon allspice**
2 teaspoons salt	
¹/₄ teaspoon pepper	*Gravy:*
2 tablespoons butter or margarine	**1¹/₄ cups pan drippings**
1 bouillon cube	**2 tablespoons all-purpose flour**
¹/₂ cup boiling water	**¹/₄ cup cold water**
2 carrots, sliced	**3/₄ cup cream or milk**

Rub meat with salt and pepper.

Heat butter or margarine in Dutch oven or heavy kettle. Add meat and brown well on all sides. Remove from heat.

Dissolve bouillon cube in water. Pour into pan; add carrots, onions and allspice. Cover closely and let simmer gently until meat is tender, about 1¹/₂–2 hours. Or, roast uncovered in moderate oven (325°) about 30–35 minutes per pound. Remove meat to hot serving platter.

Makes 6 servings.

Gravy:

Strain and measure pan drippings; add water if necessary to make 1¹/₄ cups and return to pan.

Blend flour and ¹/₄ cup cold water. Stir into drippings and cook, stirring, over low heat until smooth. Gradually pour in cream. Cook, stirring, until smooth and thickened.

Slice meat and serve with the gravy, Roasted Potatoes, Swedish Style, see page 73, vegetables and Pickled Fresh Cucumber, see page 84. See color picture opposite page 95.

VEAL CUTLET
À LA OSCAR
(with asparagus and Béarnaise Sauce)

KALVKOTLETT
À LA OSCAR

Many people have asked for the recipe for this dish.

You might find it served in Scandinavian restaurants in America and in many first-class restaurants in Sweden, where it is a much favored dish. That is because the flavors of the delicate sauce, the meat and asparagus blend so well together.

$1^3/_4$–2 pounds veal tender loin or
cutlet ($1/_2$-inch thick)
1 teaspoon salt
$1/_8$ teaspoon pepper
2 tablespoons butter or margarine
1 No. 300 can of asparagus
spears ($14^1/_2$ ounce)
$1/_2$ cup cooked lobster meat,
optional

Béarnaise Sauce:
3 tablespoons good vinegar
2 sprigs parsley
$1/_2$ teaspoon salt
$1/_4$ teaspoon sugar
8 crushed peppercorns
2 tablespoons minced onion
2 tablespoons drippings from fried
meat
2 egg yolks
$1/_2$ cup soft butter, preferably
unsalted
1 tablespoon chopped parsley

Cut meat into 4 serving portions, pound lightly; season with salt and pepper.

Melt butter or margarine in large frying pan. Brown meat on both sides (if using veal cutlets, cover and simmer 10–15 minutes or until tender). Keep meat warm.

Heat asparagus and lobster, if used, by placing cans in hot (but not boiling) water.

Béarnaise Sauce:

Mix vinegar, parsley, salt, sugar, peppercorns (dash of pepper will do if you do not have any peppercorns) and onion in a small saucepan. Cook over low heat until liquid is reduced to half its quantity ($1^1/_2$ tablespoons). This can be prepared ahead of time.

Measure drippings from fried meat, cook, if necessary, until reduced to two tablespoons.

Put vinegar mixture and egg yolks into top of double boiler, add 1 tablespoon of soft butter and gradually beat in reduced drippings.

Place pan over hot, but not boiling water, and stir sauce briskly until thickened.

Remove from heat and beat in bit by bit remaining butter and parsley. Sauce should have consistency of Hollandaise Sauce.

Arrange meat on hot serving platter.

Drain asparagus and pile a few spears on each piece of meat, place the rest around meat.

Spoon Béarnaise Sauce over middle of asparagus and top with lobster if used. Serve remaining sauce separately.

Serve with Cheese-Potato Wedges, see page 71, and Mixed Salad, see page 82.

Makes 4 servings.

BRAISED VEAL BIRDS   KALVRULADER

This is one of my favorite veal dishes. Besides being very tasty, it is easy to prepare and can be cooked ahead of time.

$1^1/_2$ pounds veal cutlets	8 thin slices cheese
$1/_4$ cup all-purpose flour	2 tablespoons salad oil
$1/_4$ teaspoon salt	$1/_2$ cup bouillon or boiling water
$1/_4$ teaspoon pepper	$1/_4$ cup cream or milk
8 thin slices boiled ham	

Have your butcher pound the meat very thin and flat (as for scallopini). Cut meat into 8 uniform pieces about 4×8 inches.

Mix flour, salt and pepper on a piece of waxed paper. Coat meat on both sides with this mixture.

Place a slice of ham and cheese on each piece of meat. Roll up and secure with toothpicks or string.

Heat oil in heavy skillet. Add meat and brown quickly on all sides. Add bouillon or water, cover closely and simmer until meat is tender, about 30 minutes.

Lift Veal Birds from pan. Add cream or milk to liquid in pan and let cook a few minutes, season to taste. Depending upon saltiness of ham and cheese the exact amount for seasoning is difficult to give.

Remove toothpicks or string, place Veal Birds in deep serving dish and pour gravy over.

Serve with lingonberries, or with Creamed Potatoes from Skåne, see page 72, and Mixed Salad, see page 82.

Makes 4 servings.

VEAL CHICKENS
KALVKYCKLING

Prepare as for Braised Veal Birds, see page 109, but instead of the meat-cheese filling, use a mixture of $^1/_3$ cup butter and $^1/_3$ cup chopped parsley.

VEAL CHOPS WITH MUSHROOMS

PANERADE KALVKOTLETTER
MED CHAMPINJONER

4 veal chops or 1 large veal
   cutlet (about 2 pounds)
1 teaspoon salt
$^1/_4$ teaspoon pepper
2 tablespoons lemon juice
1 egg, slightly beaten

$^1/_4$ pound mushrooms
2 tablespoons chopped parsley
$^1/_4$ cup fine, dry bread crumbs
$^1/_4$ cup olive or salad oil
1 cup cream or milk

If you use a veal cutlet, cut it into four pieces.

Sprinkle meat with salt, pepper and lemon juice; let stand for a few minutes. Brush both sides with egg.

Wipe mushrooms with damp paper towel. Chop 4 of them very fine, the rest to ordinary size.

Mix finely chopped mushrooms with parsley and fine, dry bread crumbs. Dip meat into crumb mixture, coating well on both sides.

Heat oil in large skillet; add meat and cook slowly until golden brown on both sides. If chops are not tender by then, cover and simmer until tender. Remove chops and keep warm.

Put remaining chopped mushrooms into frying pan and toss around for a few minutes. Add cream or milk and simmer until thickened. Season to taste and pour over chops.

Serve immediately with Baked Potatoes with Caraway Seed, see page 71, and String Beans au Gratin, see page 76.

Makes 4 servings.

LOIN OF PORK WITH PRUNES

PLOMMONSPÄCKAD
FLÄSKKARRÉ

A good Swedish way of preparing pork.

10 prunes, halved and pitted
$^1/_2$ cup warm water
4 pounds loin of pork

2 teaspoons salt
$^1/_2$ teaspoon pepper
$^1/_4$ teaspoon ginger, optional

110

Loin of Pork Stuffed with Prunes
Plommonspäckad fläskkarré

Soak halved prunes in warm water for $^1/_2$ hour. Drain, saving liquid. Insert prunes deep into meat, see picture above.

Rub meat with salt, pepper and ginger if desired. Tie roast with string into shape if necessary.

Place meat in small roasting pan and roast uncovered in slow oven (325°) 40–45 minutes per pound. Remove meat to hot serving platter; remove string and cut away back bone. Add prune juice to drippings and cook, stirring a few minutes. Strain liquid and serve as gravy.

If *thick gravy* is preferred, strain drippings into measuring cup and skim off the fat. Return 2 tablespoons of the fat to the pan. Blend in 2 tablespoons flour and stir over low heat until lightly browned.

Measure drippings and add water to make 1 cup liquid. Stir into flour mixture and add $^1/_2$ cup milk or cream, cook, stirring, until smooth and thick. Remove from heat and season with $^1/_2$ teaspoon salt, 1 teaspoon red currant jelly and dash of ginger.

Slice meat and serve with gravy, Baked Potatoes with Caraway Seed, see page 71, and Spiced Red Cabbage, see page 77.

Makes 6 servings.

111

PORK LOIN IN ASPIC

FLÄSKALADÅB

This is a very popular dish in Sweden's most southern state, Skåne, where it is frequently served with the Smörgåsbord. You will always find it there during the Christmas season. During the hot summer months in America, it makes an excellent main course, served with Pickled Red Beets, or a Mixed Salad. Many people like a sour cream dressing seasoned with mustard, and some liquid from the pickled beets with this dish. Since pork is often on sale at bargain prices, this makes an economical dish as well as an easy one on the homemaker.

$3^1/_2$–4 pounds lean loin of pork	$1/_2$ teaspoon peppercorns
5 cups water	1 clove garlic
1 peeled onion	2 bay leaves
2 carrots	$1/_3$ cup white vinegar
3 stalks celery	1 teaspoon Worcestershire sauce
1 tablespoon salt	$1^1/_2$ teaspoons Soya sauce
8 whole cloves	2 envelopes unflavored gelatin

Put meat into a large kettle; add water and bring to the boiling point. Skim surface until clear. Add remaining ingredients except Soya sauce and gelatin. Cover tightly and bring slowly to the boiling point. Reduce heat and simmer for $1^1/_2$ hours, or until pork is tender.

Remove meat from stock and cool. Cut meat away from bone and slice, but keep slices together so they will look like a whole piece of meat.

Add Soya sauce to stock. Strain stock through several layers of cheese cloth or a thin, wet tea towel. Cool stock. Skim off all fat collected on the surface and return stock to kettle.

Sprinkle gelatin over stock and heat until gelatin dissolves.

Pour $1/_2$ cup of stock into bottom of a $10 \times 5 \times 3$ inch loaf pan. Arrange slices of stuffed olives, pimiento, cooked carrots and small sprigs of greens over gelatin in loaf pan. Chill until almost set. Place meat, fat side down, in pan. Pour remaining gelatin mixture over meat and chill until firm.

Unmold and garnish with crisp greens.

Makes 6 servings.

Keeps very well if refrigerated.

PORK BIRDS FLÄSKRULADER

A very popular dish in Sweden, especially among youngsters. Inexpensive and easy to prepare.

8 prunes
2/3 cup lukewarm water
1 small apple
2 teaspoons salt — *Gravy:*
1/4 teaspoon pepper — 2 tablespoons all-purpose flour
1/4 teaspoon ginger — 1/2 cup cream
8 thin slices lean pork or ham — salt
   steaks (about 4 × 8-inch pieces) — pepper
1 tablespoon butter or margarine — 1 tablespoon tomato catsup

Soak prunes in lukewarm water 15–20 minutes. Remove pits from prunes. Return pits to water and set this aside.

Peel apple and slice thinly.

Mix salt, pepper and ginger together.

Spread meat slices on a board and sprinkle with half amount of mixed spices. Place one prune and a few apple slices at one end of each meat slice and roll up; fasten with toothpicks. Season outside with remaining spices.

Melt butter or margarine in chicken fryer or heavy skillet with cover. Brown meat evenly on all sides (about 10 minutes).

Add the prune water, discarding pits. Cover pan tightly and cook over low heat 30–35 minutes, or until tender.

Remove Pork Birds and pull out toothpicks, keep meat warm.

Serve with gravy (see below), Spiced Red Cabbage, see page 77, Baked Potatoes with Caraway Seed, see page 71, and Apple Salad, see page 84.

Makes 4 servings.

Gravy:

Shake flour with cream in a covered jar. Stir into pan in which Pork Birds were cooked. Cook gravy until smooth. Season to taste with salt, pepper and tomato catsup. Pour gravy over Pork Birds.

PORK OR BACON PANCAKE

$3/4$ cup sifted all-purpose flour
$3/4$ teaspoon salt
2 cups milk
2 eggs
$1/2$ pound lightly salted side pork or $1/2$ pound bacon

Sift flour and salt into bowl. Add $1/2$ cup of the milk. Beat until smooth. Add eggs and remaining milk and beat well.

Cube pork or bacon and fry in skillet or omelet pan. Remove meat to absorbent paper. Drain all but about 2 tablespoons of fat from frying pan. Return drained meat to pan if it is a suitable type to go into the oven; if not, pour 2 tablespoons fat into an 8-inch pie plate, add meat.

Stir batter and pour over meat. Bake in moderate oven (350°) about 35 minutes, or until set and nicely brown. Cool a few minutes before serving.

Cut pancake into sections and serve with lingonberries.

Makes 3–4 servings.

ROASTED SPARERIBS

4 small or 2 large sides spareribs (about 4 pounds)
1 tablespoon salt
$1/2$ teaspoon ginger
$1/2$ teaspoon pepper

3–4 tart apples
20 prunes
1–2 beef bouillon cubes
$1^1/2$ cups water

Have sparerib bones cracked into serving size pieces.

Combine seasonings and rub into meat. Bake meat on broiler rack in pan in moderate oven (350°) for $3/4$ hour. Remove ribs and rack from broiler pan. Pour off fat.

Peel, core and slice apples. Rinse prunes and remove pits.

Spread apples and prunes in bottom of broiler pan. Place spareribs, inner side up, on top of fruit.

Dissolve bouillon cubes in water; pour over spareribs.

Bake in moderate oven (350°) for $1/2$ hour. Turn ribs. Increase heat to 400° and bake 20 minutes longer, or until ribs are crisp and golden brown.

Remove ribs from pan; cut into servings of 2 or 3 ribs each, using kitchen shears. Remove fruit and drain. Strain pan drippings and use to make gravy.

To make gravy, see recipe, page 111 for Thick Gravy under Loin of Pork with Prunes.

114

Serve ribs warm as a main course with the fruit and gravy, and with Spiced Red Cabbage, see page 77; or cold as a Smörgåsbord dish

Variations:
Rub seasonings into meat. Spread fruits on inside of ribs. Roll and tie securely. Bake about 2 hours, until meat is brown and tender. Remove spareribs from pan and carve. Strain pan juice for gravy.
Makes 6 servings.

PORK CHOPS
PIQUANT

FLÄSKKOTLETT
PIKANT

6 large, lean pork chops or
  6 slices of ham steaks
1 teaspoon salt
$1/8$ teaspoon pepper
$3/4$ cup water
1 bouillon cube
$1/2$ pound mushrooms
4 slices bacon

$3/4$ cup chopped onion
2 tablespoons all-purpose flour
$11/2$ teaspoons paprika
$3/4$ cup cream
2 tablespoons tomato catsup
$1/2$ teaspoon salt
  dash of pepper

Sprinkle chops or ham steaks with salt and pepper. Fry in small amount of fat until golden brown on each side; place in large, shallow baking dish.

Pour water into frying pan, add bouillon cube, simmer a few minutes, stirring. Pour bouillon into small bowl and set aside.

Wipe mushrooms clean with damp paper towel, or rinse quickly under cold, running water; drain. Slice mushrooms lengthwise over pork chops.

Cut bacon into small pieces with scissors. Sauté bacon and onion for 10 minutes. Pour off excess fat.

Sprinkle mixture with flour and paprika; stir in cream and bouillon, simmer 5 minutes.

Stir in tomato catsup and taste sauce before adding salt and pepper. It should be a rich, flavorful sauce, but because of different brands of bouillon cubes and bacon the amount of seasonings may vary.

Spoon sauce over mushrooms and chops.

Bake in moderate oven (375°) 25–30 minutes.

Serve with cooked rice and Apple Salad, see page 84.

Makes 6 servings.

Fried Pork with Apple Rings and Brown Beans
Stekt fläsk med äppleringar och bruna bönor

FRIED PORK   STEKT FLÄSK

1¹/₂ pounds lightly salted, or fresh, side pork

Cut pork into ¹/₄-inch thick slices. Remove rind, or make a few gashes in rind with scissors.

Heat a skillet, add pork slices and fry until nicely brown and crisp. If fresh pork is used, sprinkle it with salt and pepper.

Serve with Onion Sauce, see page 166, and potatoes in their jackets, or with Brown Beans, Swedish Style, see page 76, and Apple Rings, see picture above.

Makes 4 servings.

For Apple Rings:

Cut unpeeled apples into ¹/₂-inch thick slices. Fry in butter or margarine over medium heat until nicely browned on both sides.

116

BOILED LAMB WITH DILL SAUCE

2 pounds boned shoulder lamb

1 quart boiling water

1 bay leaf

dill sprigs

2 teaspoons salt

8 peppercorns

5 whole allspice

Dill Sauce, see recipe, page 164

Place meat in saucepan and add boiling water. Bring to the boiling point and skim the surface until clear. Add bay leaf, dill, salt, peppercorns and allspice. Cover and simmer until meat is tender, about 1–1$^1/_2$ hours. Save stock for use in sauce.

Slice meat and arrange slices on hot serving platter. Garnish with dill; serve with Dill Sauce and boiled potatoes.

(Veal may be substituted for lamb.)

Makes 4 servings.

LAMB AND CABBAGE

FÅR I KÅL

This makes good hearty eating and is economical to prepare.

1 tablespoon butter or margarine

2 pounds boned shoulder lamb, cubed

1 tablespoon salt

$^1/_2$ teaspoon peppercorns

2 bay leaves

2 cups water

1 medium head green cabbage

chopped parsley

Melt butter or margarine in large heavy saucepan; add meat and brown well. If there seems to be too much fat, drain some off but not all – you'll want some for flavor.

Sprinkle meat with 2 teaspoons of the salt; add peppercorns, bay leaves and water. Bring to the boiling point; cover and simmer for about 15 minutes.

Trim cabbage and cut into large pieces, add to meat and sprinkle with remaining salt. Continue to cook very gently for 25–35 minutes, or until meat and cabbage are tender.

Mix cabbage and meat well. Turn into deep serving dish and sprinkle with parsley.

Serve with boiled potatoes.

Makes 4 servings.

Preparing Potato Dumplings
Beredning av kroppkakor

POTATO DUMPLINGS WITH PORK KROPPKAKOR

6 medium potatoes
1 egg yolk, beaten
$1^1/_2$ teaspoons salt
$1/_2$ cup all-purpose flour
$1/_4$ pound salt side pork or
  $1/_4$ pound bacon

$1/_4$ pound smoked ham
$1/_4$ cup chopped onion
1 tablespoon salt
13 quarts water

Wash and peel potatoes; cook in small amount salted water or steam them. Drain and mash – not with an electric mixer though, they get too sticky – let cool. (You should have about 3 cups of mashed potatoes.)

Mix egg yolk and salt into potatoes. Turn onto floured board; gradually add flour, working mixture into a dough with palms of hands. Amount of flour depends on how moist potatoes are – use more or less than $1/_2$ cup, enough to make the dough smooth and easy to handle. Shape dough into a long roll and cut into 10 slices. Make a depression in each slice, see picture above.

Cube pork and ham finely; fry quickly in skillet. Remove meat from skillet and cook onion in the same fat until golden brown; mix with meat

Place 1 tablespoon meat mixture in the depression in each potato slice. Using floured hands, fold potato around meat and shape into round dumplings.

Add salt to water; bring to the boiling point. Drop dumplings into water and boil gently about 4–5 minutes; drain.

Serve immediately with melted butter; or cool and cut in half and fry in butter until golden brown.

Makes 4–5 servings.

GOURMET LAMB
LAMMGRYTA GOURMET

2 pounds lean boned shoulder
  lamb or 2 pounds lamb cutlets
1/4 cup all-purpose flour
1 tablespoon salt
1/4 teaspoon pepper
1 tablespoon shortening
3 cloves garlic
1 10 1/2-ounce can consommé or
  1 1/4 cups water and 2 bouillon
  cubes

1/4 cup tomato paste
2 bay leaves
2 stalks celery, cut-up
1 medium onion, quartered
1 No. 303 can whole onions
  (1 pound)
1 thirteen-ounce can
  baby carrots
1 No. 303 can small new potatoes
  (1 pound)

Cut meat into large cubes.

Mix flour with salt and pepper; coat meat with this mixture.

Melt fat in a heavy skillet or chicken fryer; brown meat on all sides.

Add garlic, consommé or water and bouillon cubes, tomato paste, bay leaves, celery and onion.

Cover and cook for 30 minutes over low heat.

Open cans and drain vegetables.

Remove meat from frying pan; place layers of meat, onions, carrots and potatoes in a 2 1/2 quart casserole dish.

Pour sauce through a sieve over mixture in casserole; cover.

Bake in hot oven (425°) 40 minutes.

Sprinkle with chopped parsley and serve with Mixed Salad, see page 82.

Makes 4 servings.

Roast Leg of Lamb with Whole Fried Onions
and Sautéed Mushrooms
Lammstek med helstekt lök och champinjoner

ROAST LEG OF LAMB

LAMMSTEK

4–4^1/$_2$-pounds leg of lamb
2 teaspoons salt
^{1}/$_4$ teaspoon pepper
1 cup coffee with sugar
   and cream*

Gravy:
2 cups mixture of pan drippings
   and cream or milk
2 tablespoons all-purpose flour
1 teaspoon red currant jelly

Rub meat with salt and pepper.

Roast in moderate oven (350°) about 1^1/$_2$ hours. Pour coffee with cream and sugar into pan. Roast about 1 more hour, basting occasionally. When meat is done, remove to hot platter and keep warm.

* The coffee will remove any mutton flavor there may be in the lamb and it imparts a wonderful flavor to the gravy.

120

Gravy:

Strain pan drippings and skim off fat. Return 2 tablespoons fat to roasting pan.

Measure drippings and add cream or milk to make 2 cups liquid.

Blend flour into fat in pan and stir over low heat until lightly browned. Gradually stir in the 2 cups liquid. Cook, stirring, until smooth and thickened. Remove from heat and add red currant jelly.

Slice meat and serve with the gravy and suitable vegetables, see picture beside, such as Browned Potatoes, see page 73, Whole Fried Onions, see page 74, Sautéed Mushrooms, see page 37.

Makes 4–5 servings.

ROAST CHICKEN WITH GRAVY, SWEDISH STYLE   STEKT KYCKLING

The chickens roasted this way will be very juicy and flavorful and the gravy superb! They are also very nice chilled.

2 small roasting chickens, about	*Gravy:*
2–2¹/₂ pounds each	**2 tablespoons fat from drippings**
¹/₂ lemon	**1 tablespoon all-purpose flour**
2 teaspoons salt	**1¹/₃ cups mixture of drippings**
¹/₈ teaspoon pepper	**and cream**
1 bunch parsley	**chicken livers**
3 tablespoons butter or margarine	**¹/₂ teaspoon salt**
¹/₄ cup water	**¹/₈ teaspoon pepper**
	¹/₂ teaspoon red currant jelly,
	optional

Clean chickens; singe, remove pin feathers; wash and dry thoroughly. Rub inside chickens with lemon; rub inside and out with salt and pepper.

Place parsley and 1 tablespoon of the butter in the cavities. Coat outside of birds with 1 tablespoon butter; truss.

Melt remaining tablespoon of butter in a Dutch oven on top of stove. Brown chickens slowly on all sides, add water, cover closely and simmer gently for ¹/₂ hour or until tender.

121

Roast Chicken, Swedish Style
Stekt kyckling

When chickens are done, remove to hot platter and strain drippings into measuring cup for use in gravy, let stand a few minutes until fat floats to the top.

Gravy:

Pour fat from drippings into roasting pan. Blend in flour. Cook, stirring, until lightly brown.

Add cream to strained drippings to make $1^1/_3$ cups liquid. Gradually stir into flour mixture. Chop the raw chicken liver and add to sauce with salt, pepper and jelly; cook until smooth and thickened.

Split chickens and serve with the gravy, Browned Potatoes, see page 73, Mixed Salad, see page 82, and Pickled Fresh Cucumber, see page 84.

See picture above.

Makes 4 servings.

122

ROAST GOOSE
STEKT GÅS

*In the southern part of Sweden, people are extremely fond of good food,
and they spend much time preparing and eating their many specialities.
November the eleventh is a feast day called "Mårten Gås" and is traditionally
celebrated with a Roast Goose dinner.*

1 young goose, 10–12 pounds	*Gravy:*
1/2 lemon	1 1/2 cups pan drippings (or
2 teaspoons salt	drippings and consommé)
dash of pepper	1 tablespoon corn starch
4–5 apples, quartered	1/4 cup water
20 prunes	salt
	pepper

Clean goose, singe, wash and dry thoroughly. Rub inside and out with
lemon, salt and pepper.

Stuff cavity loosely with apples and prunes. Fold skin back over neck
and fasten with a poultry pin. Truss and place on a rack in an open roasting
pan, breast side up. Roast in moderate oven (350°) until tender, about
2 1/2 hours. If goose is very fat, pour off some fat from pan during roasting.
Test doneness by moving a drumstick. When just about done, prop oven
door slightly open to crisp skin. Remove goose to hot platter and keep warm.

Gravy:

Strain pan drippings into measuring cup, skim off fat. Return 1 1/2 cups
liquid to roasting pan. Blend corn starch with water, pour into pan liquid
and cook, stirring until smooth and thickened. Simmer 3–4 minutes and
season with salt and pepper.

Serve with a garnish of Rosy Apple Slices and whole cooked prunes.

Serve goose (discard stuffing) with gravy, Browned Potatoes, see page 73,
and Spiced Red Cabbage, see page 77.

Makes 6 servings.

Rosy Apple Slices:

Mix 2 cups sugar with 1 cup water, 1 teaspoon vinegar, 1/4 cup red
cinnamon candies and a few drops red food coloring. Bring to the boiling point
and simmer 5 minutes. Cut 5 medium, firm cooking apples into slices and
remove cores. Poach the apple slices, a few at a time, in syrup until tender,
about 5–8 minutes. If slices are thick, turn carefully once during cooking.
When tender, lift slices from the syrup and drain on a cookie sheet.

CHICKEN ASPIC

HÖNSALADÅB

This is a favorite dish and a must on a well-planned Smörgåsbord (see color picture of Smörgåsbord between pp.14 and 15. Since it should be made a day ahead of time, it will naturally become a favorite for the hostess as well. I have found this dish extremely popular among my American friends as a main course during the hot-weather season.

1 5-pounds stewing chicken	1 tablespoon lemon juice
6 cups water	1 teaspoon peppercorns
1 medium onion, quartered	1 tablespoon salt
3 stalks celery	2 envelopes unflavored gelatin
5 sprigs parsley or 2 scallions	$1/4$ cup cold water
2 bay leaves	2 stiffly beaten egg whites

Put cleaned chicken into large saucepan; add water, vegetables and seasonings. Bring to the boiling point; skim surface until clear from particles. Cover chicken and simmer gently until tender (about 2 hours). Cool chicken in stock.

Remove chicken and strain stock (there should be about 4 cups). Return stock to pan.

Soften gelatin in cold water and add to stock; stir in egg whites (they'll clarify the stock). Heat mixture slowly, stirring constantly, until it starts to boil. Remove from heat, cover and let stand for 10 minutes. Strain through a sieve that has been lined with thick layers of cheese cloth, or through a wet tea towel. Chill until syrupy.

Brush a 2 quart mold, or a mixing bowl, with oil. Pour in $1/2$ cup of the gelatin and swirl mold around to coat inside. Chill until set.

Line the mold with slices of stuffed olives, pimiento and thin slices of chicken which have been dipped in gelatin mixture. Spoon some of the remaining gelatin into mold to coat sides over olives, pimiento and chicken. Chill until set.

Slice or cube remaining chicken and arrange in mold. Pour remaining gelatin over chicken pieces. (If gelatin has become too thick, place over low heat for a few minutes.) Chill mold over night.

Unmold aspic on platter. Garnish with celery tops or watercress. Serve with mayonnaise, thinned with sour cream and seasoned with curry.

Makes 6 servings.

SWEDISH MEATBALLS

Probably the most famous of all Swedish meat dishes. What is typically Swedish is that the recipe calls for mashed, cold potatoes, which give meatballs a light consistency. Most recipes of this particular dish, and there are hundreds, are handed down from mother to daughter. The following recipe is served as a meat course, therefore the meatballs are rather large. For the small delicate ones, served with the Smörgåsbord, see page 35.

$1/2$ cup grated or finely chopped
    onion
1 tablespoon shortening
1 pound ground beef (round
    steak or chuck)
$1/2$ pound ground, lean pork
1 cup mashed or grated, cooked,
    cold potatoes (loosely packed)
$1/4$ cup fine, dry bread crumbs

$2^1/2$ teaspoons salt
$1/4$ teaspoon pepper
$1/2$ cup cream
$1/4$ cup water
1 egg

Gravy:
1 cup cream or milk
1 tablespoon all-purpose flour

For best meatballs select meat yourself and have it ground. The fresher the meat is ground, the better the meatballs.

Sauté onion in fat for 5 minutes. Place in large mixing bowl with remaining ingredients. Mix until smooth.

Shape into balls, using a tablespoon as measurement, in the wet palm of your hand; or press through pastry bag, see pictures, page 34.

Fry meatballs in plenty of hot oil or shortening ($^1/_2$ cup), shaking pan often to make balls round.

Remove each batch to hot serving dish and keep warm. Clean pan between batches if necessary, reserving fat.

When all meatballs are fried, blend cream or milk into flour and pour into pan juice.

Stir and cook until thickened, season with salt and pepper.

Strain gravy over meatballs.

Makes about 35 meatballs.

Serve with Mashed Potatoes, see page 72, or macaroni, Molded Cucumber Salad, see page 81, or lingonberries.

Makes 4 servings.

HAMBURGER À LA LINDSTRÖM

This dish is highly estimated among my friends in America. These Hamburgers are very juicy and tasty and make a wonderful lunch served on toast with a fried egg on top.

1¹/₂ pounds ground round steak	¹/₄ cup cream
2 egg yolks	³/₄ cup finely chopped pickled beets
³/₄ cup mashed potatoes	¹/₂ cup finely chopped onion
2 teaspoons salt	¹/₄ cup capers, chopped
¹/₄ teaspoon pepper	

Combine meat, egg yolks, mashed potatoes, salt and pepper. Stir in cream gradually. Mix well.

Carefully mix in beets, onion and capers.

Shape into patties about ¹/₂ inch thick and fry quickly on both sides until done.

Place patties on hot serving platter. Serve immediately, with Cheese-Potato Wedges, see page 71, and Mixed Salad, see page 82. Or serve each patty on a slice of white toast with a fried egg on top.

SWEDISH HAMBURGERS

(with fried onions and cream gravy)

¹/₃ cup fine dry bread crumbs	1 pound, lean, ground pork
1 tablespoon salt	1 egg
¹/₂ teaspoon paprika	2 tablespoons chopped parsley or
¹/₄ teaspoon pepper	scallions
¹/₂ cup water	¹/₂ cup butter or margarine
¹/₂ cup cream	3 medium onions
	1 cup cream or top milk

Soak bread crumbs and seasonings in water and cream for 10 minutes.

Add ground meat, egg and chopped parsley or scallions; mix until well blended.

Shape meat mixture into 8 round flat patties.

Melt half amount of butter or margarine in large skillet, fry patties about 4–5 minutes on each side on medium heat. Place on warm serving platter and keep warm.

Peel and slice onions thinly; sauté in remaining butter or margarine until soft and golden brown (about 12–15 minutes).

Spoon onions over hamburgers.

Pour cream or milk into frying pan, cook stirring a few minutes until it starts to thicken, season with salt and pepper. Pour over hamburgers.

Serve with Mashed Potatoes, see page 72, and Apple Salad, see page 84. Makes 4 servings.

STUFFED CABBAGE LOAF — HEL KÅLDOLMA

These two following cabbage recipes are good, hearty winter dishes, very much appreciated by the men in the family.

1 medium head green cabbage

Stuffing:

1 egg

$3/4$ cup cold mashed potatoes

2 teaspoons salt

$1/4$ teaspoon pepper

1 teaspoon Worcestershire sauce

$1/4$ cup finely chopped onion

$2/3$ cup milk

$1/2$ pound ground lean pork

$1/2$ pound ground lean beef

1 $10^1/_2$-ounce can undiluted consommé

1 tablespoon soft butter or margarine

Discard wilted leaves and remove core of cabbage. Plunge into large kettle of boiling salted water. Boil 5–7 minutes. Remove from kettle and place on several layers of paper towels. Separate leaves carefully to keep them whole. (If they do not separate easily, return cabbage to kettle and boil a few minutes longer.)

Stuffing: Mix together egg, potatoes, seasonings, onion and milk until very smooth. Add ground meat and stir until well blended.

Butter a roasting pan; place bases of leaves in the center, overlapping each other so that rounded edges of leaves are hanging over edge of roasting pan. Shape meat stuffing into a loaf and wrap cabbage leaves around.

Pour consommé over loaf and spread top with butter or margarine.

Bake in moderate oven (350°) $1^1/_2$ hours, basting occasionally.

If cabbage browns too quickly, cover with aluminium foil.

Serve with brown gravy made from drippings in pan, boiled potatoes and lingonberries.

Makes 6 servings.

127

STUFFED CABBAGE LEAVES

KÅLDOLMAR

Although you will find this dish served in different ways in all countries along the Baltic Sea, many Swedes claim it as one of their most traditional dishes. It is especially good, when the cabbage is new.

Stuffing:
see recipe for Stuffed Cabbage
Loaf, page 127

1 medium head green cabbage

2 tablespoons shortening
1 tablespoon dark corn syrup
or brown sugar
1 10¹/₂-ounce can consommé
or tomato soup

Prepare meat and cabbage stuffing as in recipe for Stuffed Cabbage Loaf, see page 127.

Remove coarse middle veins from each leaf. Spoon 2 tablespoons of meat stuffing on each flat cabbage leaf near the stem end, roll stem end over mixture once; fold in sides, see picture beside. Brush edge of leaf with egg white to seal. Finish rolling and fasten with toothpicks.

There are 2 ways of cooking this dish. The real oldfashioned Swedish way, method one, and one more simplified.

Method one: Melt shortening in chicken fryer or Dutch oven; add rolls a few at a time and brown on all sides, sprinkle with corn syrup or brown sugar (if you do not have a large frying pan, you will have to repeat the frying process twice). Pour in consommé, cover and cook over low heat for about 1 hour or until tender. Remove to hot serving dish.

To make gravy: Shake 1¹/₂ cups of cream or milk with 4 teaspoons flour and stir into pan juice.

Cook, stirring until smooth, season to taste and pour over Stuffed Cabbage Leaves.

Method two: For this method you do not need to fasten with toothpicks.

Place Stuffed Cabbage Leaves in buttered casserole dish. Dilute tomato soup after directions on the can and pour over leaves. Cover dish and bake in moderate oven (350°) for 1¹/₄ hours or until tender.

Serve with Mashed Potatoes, see page 72, and Mixed Salad, see page 82. Makes 6 servings.

Variation:
Instead of mashed potatoes and onion, you can use rice in the stuffing. Cook ¹/₄ cup rice in 1 cup water until tender; cool.

Add egg, seasonings, milk and meat and stir until well blended.

128

Preparing Stuffed Cabbage Leaves
Beredning av kåldolmar

FRIED CALF'S LIVER WITH CREAM SAUCE

A favorite dish among many people.

1 pound calf's liver
$1/4$ cup all-purpose flour
2 teaspoons salt
$1/4$ teaspoon pepper
3 tablespoons bacon drippings or butter
1 cup cream

Remove skin and membrane from liver. Cut into 4 slices.
Mix flour with salt and pepper.
Dredge liver slices in seasoned flour.

129

Heat fat in frying pan. Fry liver 2 minutes on each side; be careful not to overcook liver, then it will loose its delicacy.

Stir in cream, bring to the boiling point, turn liver and cover pan; cook gently for 5 minutes.

If you wish to serve onions with liver, sauté 2 large sliced onions in 2 tablespoons of fat, remove from pan and keep warm, while cooking liver.

Serve liver with Mashed Potatoes, see page 72, Spiced Red Cabbage, see page 77, and lingonberries or Pickled Fresh Cucumber, see page 84.

Makes 4 servings.

FRIED SWEETBREADS WITH MUSHROOMS AND BACON

STEKT KALVBRÄSS MED SVAMP OCH BACON

There will always be a time when you want to serve something especially good, something you do not get at everybody else's house. If you like sweetbreads, and most people do, try this recipe. It is a wonderful combination.

2 pairs of large sweetbreads
(about 2 pounds)
1 quart boiling water
1 tablespoon salt
1 tablespoon lemon juice
$1/4$ cup fine, dry bread crumbs
2 teaspoons salt

$1/4$ teaspoon pepper
$3/4$ pound mushrooms
1 tablespoon butter or margarine
8 slices bacon
$1/3$ cup butter (preferably no
substitute)

Soak sweetbreads in cold water for 1 hour; drain.

Put into saucepan with boiling water, salt and lemon juice, bring to the boiling point; simmer for 18 minutes.

Remove sweetbreads from stock. Cool stock and put sweetbreads back into cold stock (you can keep them refrigerated over night this way). Keep them in stock until ready to prepare.

Trim away membranes and tubes and cut into $3/4$-inch thick slices.

Mix bread crumbs with salt and pepper; coat slices with this mixture.

Let stand for a while to harden coating. (This far the sweetbreads can be prepared ahead of time.)

Fried Sweetbreads with Mushrooms and Bacon
Stekt kalvbräss med svamp och bacon

Clean mushrooms by wiping them with a damp paper towel. Cut into halves or leave whole; place in saucepan with butter or margarine, sprinkle with salt and pepper; cover and simmer 5–8 minutes (can be made ahead of time).

Broil bacon slices until crisp; drain and keep warm.

Melt $1/3$ cup of butter in large skillet; when golden in color, add sweetbreads.

Fry quickly 3–4 minutes on each side, or until crisp and golden brown. (Add more butter if necessary, sweetbreads should not stick to pan.)

Arrange in the middle of a hot serving platter, with bacon on one side and mushrooms on the other, see picture above.

Serve with Broiled Tomatoes, see page 84, and a tossed salad.

For a more substantial meal, serve with rice.

Makes 4 servings.

FRESH BEEF TONGUE WITH
MUSHROOM SAUCE

1 beef tongue, about 3 pounds	5 whole cloves
2 quarts boiling water	2 bay leaves
2 tablespoons salt	1 carrot, sliced
1 teaspoon black peppercorns	1 onion, sliced

Place tongue in saucepan and pour in boiling water. Bring to the boiling point and remove all the scum from the surface. Add remaining ingredients and simmer until a fork pierces tongue easily, about $2-2^1/_2$ hours.

Let tongue cool 1 hour in liquid. Remove tongue and pull off skin and trim off thick end where small bones are apparent. Return tongue to liquid until ready to serve.

At serving time, remove tongue from liquid, slice thinly, and arrange on serving platter. Garnish cold tongue with tomatoes and asparagus spears, and serve on the Smörgåsbord.

Serve warm tongue with Mushroom Sauce, see page 164, boiled or Mashed Potatoes, see page 72, and peas.

Makes 6 servings.

A more modern way of serving tongue is to bake it after it is cooked in moderate oven (375°) for 30 minutes, basting it frequently with a cup tomato sauce.

SWEDISH HASH

This dish is one of the most popular luncheon dishes in Sweden. It is made from leftover meat, such as a roast or a baked ham, and in its simplicity makes wholesome eating.

4 slices bacon
2 cups chopped onions (about 2 medium onions)
4 cups finely diced boiled potatoes
1 teaspoon salt
   dash of pepper
2 cups finely chopped leftover meat, or boiled ham, or fried steak

Swedish Hash
Pytt i panna

Cut bacon with scissors directly into frying pan. When crisp, drain bacon on absorbent paper, leaving fat in pan.

Add onions and sauté until golden brown: remove from pan.

Add potatoes to pan, along with a little butter or margarine if needed, and fry until golden brown.

Sprinkle with salt and pepper; add bacon, onions and meat.

Mix well by carefully turning ingredients around with a spatula.

Serve piping hot with fried eggs, pickles and tomato catsup, see picture above.

Makes 4 servings.

133

Ham Rolls
Skinkrulader

HAM ROLLS WITH CREAMED SPINACH

SKINKRULADER MED STUVAD SPENAT

A very popular dish during the summer.

8 large thin slices boiled smoked ham or Bayonne ham or Italian
 smoked, dried ham (uncooked)
Creamed Spinach, see recipe, page 23
4 eggs

Cut off rind of ham and roll up slices into rolls. Place them on a serving platter, garnished with lettuce or celery tops. See picture above.
Prepare Creamed Spinach, pour into a deep serving dish. Keep warm.
Boil eggs 8 minutes and peel. Cut eggs into halves lengthwise. Place eggs on top of spinach or between the ham rolls.
Serve with small, boiled potatoes.
Makes 4 servings.

Desserts

MODERN SWEDISH APPLE CAKE

LÄTTLAGAD ÄPPLEKAKA

When you have plenty of good baking apples, make this flavorful dessert. It will not take much time to prepare.

8 medium tart apples
1/2 cup fine, dry bread crumbs
3/4 cup brown sugar
11/2 teaspoons cinnamon
1/2 cup melted butter or margarine
1/3 cup cherry brandy, rum, sauterne or orange juice

Peel and core apples; cut into thin slices.
Mix bread crumbs, brown sugar and cinnamon together.
Butter a 5 cup baking dish. Place a layer of apples in bottom of dish, sprinkle with crumb mixture and melted butter; repeat finishing with a layer of crumbs on top. Pour brandy, or other liquid, over cake and bake in hot oven (400°) for about 25 minutes, or until apples are tender. Cool and serve with Vanilla Sauce, see page 168, or whipped cream.
Makes 4 servings.

OLD FASHIONED SWEDISH APPLE CAKE WITH VANILLA SAUCE

ÄPPLEKAKA MED VANILJSÅS

6 tart apples, peeled and cubed
1/4 cup water
1/2 cup sugar
1 slice lemon
1/2 cup butter or margarine
21/2 cups Zwieback crumbs, or stale Swedish "limpa"
11/2 teaspoons cinnamon
2 tablespoons butter or margarine

135

Decorating Swedish Applecake with confectioner's sugar
Äpplekaka dekoreras med florsocker

Combine apples, water and sugar in saucepan; add lemon slice. Bring to the boiling point; simmer until apples are tender. You should have $2^1/_2$ cups firm applesauce. Use canned applesauce if you wish.

Melt the $^1/_2$ cup butter or margarine in frying pan. Add crumbs and cinnamon and cook, stirring, over low heat until evenly browned.

Alternate layers of crumbs and applesauce in a buttered 8-inch cake pan, ending with a layer of crumbs on top. Dot with 2 tablespoons butter or margarine. Bake in a moderate oven (375°) for 25 minutes. Cool slightly.

Unmold on serving plate. Sprinkle top with confectioners' sugar, or make a pattern on the cake, see picture above, by placing a perforated paper lace doily over surface. Sprinkle with confectioners' sugar and remove carefully. Serve with ice cold Vanilla Sauce, see page 168.

Makes 4 servings.

136

FILLED BAKED APPLES

6 large baking apples

¹/₂ cup almonds, ground

¹/₂ cup sugar

1 egg white, or 2 tablespoons
water

¹/₃ cup butter or margarine

¹/₃ cup fine, dry bread crumbs

2 tablespoons sugar

1 teaspoon cinnamon

Peel and core apples.

Mix together ground almonds, the ¹/₂ cup sugar and egg white or water.
Blend until smooth.

Fill apple centers with almond paste.

Melt butter or margarine in small saucepan.

Mix together bread crumbs, sugar and cinnamon.

Swirl apples in melted butter, holding them with a fork, until well coated.
Then roll them in crumb mixture until well coated.

Set apples in buttered baking dish and bake in hot oven (425°) until
tender, about 25 minutes.

Serve with Butterscotch Sauce, see page 167, or Vanilla Sauce, see
page 168.

Makes 6 delicious servings.

APPLE DUMPLINGS

*These are the best apple dumplings I have ever eaten. Served with the
Uncooked Vanilla Sauce, it makes wonderful eating.*

Pastry:

2 cups sifted all-purpose flour

1 cup cold butter or margarine

4–5 tablespoons ice water

Filling:

8 medium tart baking apples

¹/₃ cup sugar

1 tablespoon cinnamon

2 tablespoons butter or margarine

Topping:

1 tablespoon sugar

2 tablespoons chopped almonds
or nuts

137

Preparing Apple Dumplings
Beredning av äppleknyten

Measure flour into bowl.

Cut in butter or margarine with 2 knives or pastry blender until the pieces are the size of peas.

Add water gradually, toss lightly. Collect particles and shape into a round ball between floured hands.

Chill dough for 30 minutes – makes it easier to handle.

Peel and core apples and arrange in shallow baking dish. Mix sugar and cinnamon and use to fill centers of apples. Dot with butter.

Turn chilled dough onto floured board. Roll out pastry, $^1/_4$-inch thick, and cut into 5-inch squares. Place a square over each apple and shape dough around apple and press to bottom of dish; sprinkle with sugar and chopped almonds, see picture above.

Bake in moderate oven (375°) until pastry is light brown and apples are tender, about 40 minutes.

Serve warm with well chilled whipped cream or Uncooked Vanilla Sauce, see page 168.

Makes 8 servings.

138

APPLE MERINGUE CAKE

$7/4$ cup butter or margarine
1 cup sugar
3 eggs
$13/4$ cups sifted cake flour
$11/2$ teaspoons baking powder
grated rind of 1 lemon

Cream butter or margarine with sugar until light and fluffy.
Beat in one egg at a time.
Sift dry ingredients together and add to creamed mixture: blend well.
Butter a 9-inch square cake pan and sprinkle with fine, dry bread crumbs.
Pour batter into cake pan; bake in moderate oven (350°) 35 minutes, cool.

Apple-Meringue Topping:
1 cup sugar
2 cups water
juice of 1 lemon
1 stick cinnamon
few drops red food coloring
6 cooking apples

Cook a thin syrup of sugar, water, lemon juice, cinnamon and a few
drops of red food coloring.
Peel, core and quarter apples. Drop into syrup and simmer gently until
tender, turning occasionally.
Arrange apples on cake and top with

Meringue:
$1/2$ cup egg whites
1 cup confectioners' sugar
$1/2$ teaspoon vanilla

Beat egg whites until soft peaks form.
Add gradually sugar and vanilla and beat until peaks hold stiff points.
Bake in slow oven (300°) 20 minutes.
Serve warm with ice cold, Uncooked Vanilla Sauce, see page 168, whipped
cream or ice cream.
Makes 8 servings.

SWEDISH PANCAKES
PLÄTTAR

You will find a color picture of these famous delicacies opposite p. 15, which will show you what the real Swedish ones are like, and how they are served. The even, round shape you can only get by baking the pancakes in a Swedish iron pancake pan ("plättpanna"), which usually is sold in Swedish delicatessen stores and in well-stocked department stores. Since most people are so extremely fond of these pancakes, this pan is a good investment of only a few dollars. Otherwise bake them in a heavy frying pan or on a griddle.

3 eggs	$1/4$ cup melted butter or margarine
1 cup cream	$1/4$ teaspoon salt
1 cup sifted all-purpose flour	1 tablespoon sugar
2 cups milk	

Beat eggs and cream in a mixing bowl, sift in flour and beat batter until smooth. Add milk gradually; stir in melted fat, salt and sugar.

Heat Swedish pancake pan, frying pan or griddle, brush with melted shortening. (Pan should be well heated, almost hot – for electric use medium heat.)

Stir batter before adding about 2 tablespoons into sections of pan (or pour from a small pitcher). Lift up pan and turn it around to make batter cover as large an area as possible (the thinner the pancakes will be).

When surface starts to bubble and get dry, cut pancakes loose from sides with thin knife or a small spatula. Turn quickly to cook on other side until golden brown.

Pile pancakes on top of each other and transfer pile to hot serving platter (keep this over pan with boiling water).

Repeat baking procedure until batter is finished.

Pancakes are best if served immediately. If they have to be kept for some length of time, brush top layers with melted butter, keep airtight by wrapping platter in aluminum foil.

Reheat in oven or over hot water.

Serve with sugar, lingonberry jam and light cream or milk, if you so wish.

Makes 4 servings.

SOUFFLÉ OMELET
SOUFFLE OMELETT

When you want to prepare something especially good for a few friends, try this recipe which a chef from a famous restaurant in Stockholm once gave me.

The omelet is easiest to handle, if made from not more than 4 eggs at a time.

Count per person:

2 eggs

1 tablespoon sugar

Separate eggs; beat egg whites until they hold stiff peaks; gradually add sugar and beat again until they are very stiff.

Fold carefully in egg yolks, and stir just until blended.

Melt 3 tablespoons butter (not margarine) in large, heavy skillet or omelet pan.

Pour mixture into pan, cover; bake slowly on low heat, moving pan in circle over heat, so that omelet gets baked evenly. This takes just a few minutes.

Roll or fold omelet and let slide down on heated serving plate. Pour a few drops brandy or rum over and sprinkle with sugar. Serve immediately.

CRISP CREAM WAFFLES   FRASVÅFFLOR

Crisp Cream Waffles are served traditionally in Sweden on the 25th of March, the day of the Virgin Mary's conception – "Marie Bebådelsedag" in Swedish. The waffles are either served as a dessert or with coffee in the afternoon. They are delicious and easy to prepare. If any batter is left over, it can be used the next day with a few tablespoons of water added to it.

1³/₄ cups heavy cream

1¹/₂ cups sifted cake flour

¹/₂ cup ice water

3 tablespoons melted butter or margarine

1 teaspoon vanilla

¹/₂ teaspoon salt

Beat cream until stiff. Sift in flour; add ice water, blend well. Fold in melted butter, vanilla and salt.

Bake in preheated waffle baker on medium heat. Use about ¹/₂ cup of batter for each batch and bake until golden brown.

If waffle baker has not been in use for a long time, brush it with melted shortening, otherwise this is not necessary.

Serve immediately sprinkled with sugar and cinnamon, or with jam.

Makes about 8 waffles.

Tracing circles with saucer

Markera ringar med ett
tefat som mall

Spreading batter thinly to the edge of the circles

Bred ut degen tunt i
ringarna

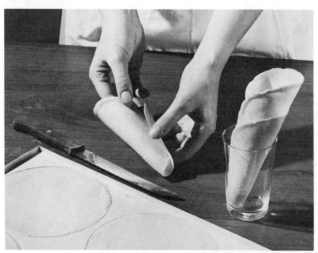

Shaping the warm cakes into cones

Forma kakorna till strutar

Cornucopias with filling
Fyllda strutar

CORNUCOPIAS   FYLLDA STRUTAR

2/3 cup sugar   1/4 teaspoon salt
2 eggs, slightly beaten   2/3 cup sifted all-purpose flour
1 teaspoon grated lemon rind   2 tablespoons melted butter or margarine

Add sugar to eggs gradually while beating. Beat well, about 3 minutes with electric mixer at medium speed.

Blend in lemon rind, salt and flour.

Stir in butter or margarine; mix well.

Trace 6-inch circles (use saucer or small plate as a guide) on well-buttered, floured cookie sheets, see pictures beside.

Spoon about 2 tablespoons of batter in center of each circle, and spread thinly to edge of circle with spatula.

Bake in moderate (350°) oven 4–5 minutes, or until golden brown.

Remove circles, one at a time, and shape into cones immediately. Work quickly. If circles become brittle, warm in oven to soften. Stack them in a glass so they won't unroll.

Makes 16 cones.

Store cones in tightly-covered cookie jar.

Fillings for Cornucopias

Berry Filling:

1 cup heavy cream
1 cup fresh or frozen berries or preserved lingonberries

Whip cream and fold in berries. (If frozen berries are used, drain them.
If berries are fresh, mash them and add a little sugar.) Fills 8 cones.

Chocolate Filling I:

1 cup heavy cream
1 tablespoon cocoa, sifted
1 ounce semi-sweet chocolate, grated
1 teaspoon vanilla
3 tablespoons sugar

Whip cream; fold in remaining ingredients. Fills 8 cones.

Chocolate Filling II:

$1/2$ package prepared chocolate pudding
$1/2$ cup heavy cream, whipped

Prepare pudding according to directions on package. Fold whipped
cream into cool pudding. Fills 8 cones.

FILLED CREAM PUFF RING FYLLD PETITS
CHOUX RING

*This is a truly delicious dessert, easy to make and yet very "fancy" looking.
It looks like it comes out of a famous chef's kitchen. You can make it the day
of your party or ahead of time and freeze it.*

1 cup water
$1/4$ cup butter or margarine
1 cup sifted all-purpose flour
$1/4$ teaspoon salt
4 small eggs (break eggs into glass measuring cup, shall measure 6 oz.)

144

Put water and butter or margarine in saucepan, bring to the boiling point. Remove pan from heat; add flour and salt, all at once, stirring constantly. Return to heat and cook until mixture leaves sides of pan in a smooth compact ball. Remove from heat and cool for about 1 minute.

Beat eggs slightly in the measuring cup and add gradually to cooked mixture, beating vigorously until mixture is smooth again.

Butter a cookie sheet and dust with flour. Trace around an 8-inch cake pan to make a circle. Spoon batter inside of circle to make a ring or use a pastry bag with a pastry tube inside.

Bake in hot oven (400°) for 30–40 minutes or until light and firm.

The cooled ring can be filled with ice cream, whipped cream mixed with strawberries or fresh peaches, or the following Mocha Cream.

Mocha Cream:
2 tablespoons instant coffee
3/4 cup milk
3 eggs, separated
2/3 cup sugar
   dash of salt
1 envelope unflavored gelatin
2 tablespoons cold water
3/4 cup heavy cream, whipped

Blend instant coffee and milk in top of double boiler. Heat until warm.

Mix egg yolks, half of the sugar and salt; add scalded milk, beating vigorously. Poor mixture back into pan and cook, stirring constantly, over simmering water till mixture coats a metal spoon.

Soften gelatin in water, add to warm custard and stir till dissolved. Remove from heat and cool; chill in refrigerator till mixture is beginning to set. Fold in whipped cream.

Beat egg whites till stiff. Add remaining sugar gradually and beat till meringue is stiff enough to hold a point, yet still looks moist. Fold into gelatin mixture. Chill for some hours in refrigerator, or over night.

Just before serving, cut off top of ring.

Spoon filling on bottom layer, put top over, sprinkle with confectioners' sugar or spread with chocolate icing.

Serve plain or with whipped cream.

Makes 8–10 servings.

LEMON CHIFFON PUDDING

CITRONFROMAGE

Light, good and refreshing . . .

2/3 cup milk or light cream

3 eggs, separated

2/3 cup sugar

   dash of salt

1 envelope unflavored gelatin

2 tablespoons cold water

1/4 cup lemon juice

2 teaspoons grated lemon rind

1/2 cup heavy cream, whipped

Scald milk or cream in top of double boiler.

Mix egg yolks, half of the sugar and salt; add, while stirring, to the scalded milk.

Cook mixture, stirring constantly, over simmering water till mixture coats a metal spoon.

Soften gelatin in cold water; add to warm custard, and stir until dissolved. Remove pan from heat; cool.

Add lemon juice gradually and lemon rind. Chill in refrigerator till mixture is beginning to set about 15 minutes.

Fold in whipped cream.

Beat egg whites till stiff. Add remaining sugar gradually and beat till meringue is stiff enough to hold a point, yet still looks moist. Fold meringue into gelatin mixture.

Spoon into individual serving dishes, rinsed with cold water and chill till firm. Garnish with fresh or canned fruit and whipped cream, see color picture opposite page 97.

Pudding can also be poured into an 8-inch pie shell or a graham cracker shell. It can be served plain or topped with whipped cream and a few maraschino cherries.

A delicious dessert that makes 6 servings.

FILLED LEMONS

FYLLDA CITRONER

This is a rather tart dessert, but a very good one on top of a heavy meal.

4 large lemons

1 No. 1 flat can of crushed pineapple (9 oz.)

3 bananas, chopped

1/4 cup rum

2–3 tablespoons sugar

146

Select lemons with a nice rind and wash.

To make lemons stand steady, cut off a thin slice at one end. At the other end, cut off a thicker slice and separate meat from peel with a grapefruit knife, saving juice and lemon pieces. Scoop out as much meat as possible. Remove seeds and membranes from lemons; cut into small pieces.

Mix lemon juice and pieces, crushed pineapple, bananas, rum and sugar, sweeten to taste. Chill mixture in refrigerator.

Spoon into lemon shells or serve in fruit cups.

Makes 4 servings.

ORANGE SHERBERT   APELSINGLASS

2 cups water	3 tablespoons lemon juice
1 cup sugar	$1/2$ cup sugar
2 teaspoons grated orange rind	$1/4$ cup water
1 cup orange juice	1 egg white

Boil gently 2 cups of water and 1 cup of sugar for 10 minutes. Add grated orange rind and cool.

Add the fruit juices and stir well.

Pour syrup through a sieve lined with cheesecloth into a refrigerator tray and freeze until firm about 1 hour.

Break ice into pieces into a chilled mixing bowl and beat with electric mixer or with rotary beater until smooth.

Then add a meringue, see below, and stir until well blended. Continue to freeze, stirring occasionally until it begins to set in small crystals.

Serve spooned into chilled sherbert glasses, with a cherry on top or fill into centers of canned pear halves. For extra flavor, sprinkle chilled, green curaçao liqueur over sherbert, just before serving.

To make meringue:

Boil $1/2$ cup sugar with $1/4$ cup water with a pinch of cream of tartar until it spins a light thread. (Place a drop of syrup between two fingers, separate fingers to check viscosity of syrup), or if you use a candy thermometer to 230°.

Beat this syrup gradually into the stiffly beaten egg whites and continue to beat until the meringue is cool.

Makes 6-8 servings.

ORANGE FLUFF

An inexpensive dessert, good for all occasions and not dangerous for the waistline.

4 eggs, separated	$1/2$ cup lemon juice
1 cup sugar	3 drops red food coloring
2 teaspoons grated orange rind	1 envelope unflavored gelatin
1 cup orange juice	$1/4$ cup cold water

Beat egg yolks with half amount of sugar until light and fluffy.

Add orange rind, fruit juices and food coloring; stir until well blended.

Soften gelatin in cold water, heat over boiling water until dissolved; add to orange mixture.

Chill for half an hour or until mixture begins to set, stirring occasionally.

Beat egg whites until foamy, gradually add remaining sugar and beat until meringue holds stiff but moist peaks. Fold into orange mixture.

Pour into individual serving dishes or into a $1^1/_2$ quart serving dish, rinsed with cold water.

Chill dessert until set; serve garnished with whipped cream, or with an orange slice topped with a maraschino cherry on each serving dish.

Makes 6 servings.

PINEAPPLE CHIFFON PUDDING

2 eggs, separated	2 tablespoons cold water
$1/2$ cup sugar	1 cup heavy cream, whipped
2 tablespoons lemon juice	1 cup canned, drained pineapple
$1/2$ cup pineapple juice	chunks or tidbits
1 envelope unflavored gelatin	

Beat egg yolks with half of sugar and lemon juice until well blended; add pineapple juice.

Soften gelatin in cold water and dissolve over low heat. Pour into egg mixture and blend well. Chill mixture until it is thickened but not set, about 30 minutes.

Beat egg whites until stiff, then gradually add remaining sugar and beat again until meringue holds stiff peaks.

Fold first whipped cream into thickened gelatin mixture then add meringue

and pineapple chunks. Pour into a 5 cup mold, which has been rinsed with
cold water. Chill at least 3 hours or over night, before serving.

Unmold onto serving platter and garnish with additional pineapple
pieces, blue grapes and fancy cookies.

Makes 6 servings.

RASPBERRY CREAM   HALLONKRÄM

When thoroughly chilled, this simple dessert is delicious.

1 quart raspberries	**4 tablespoons corn starch**
1–1¹/₄ cups sugar	**4 tablespoons water**
2 cups water	

Clean berries. Taste for sweetness. If they are naturally quite sweet,
use only 1 cup sugar.

Combine sugar and water; bring to the boiling point and simmer for a
few minutes. Add berries and boil gently 3–4 minutes.

Mix corn starch and water; stir into fruit and bring to the boiling point,
stirring constantly. Cook over low heat, stirring occasionally, 3–4 minutes.
Cover and cool.

Serve with cream or milk.

Makes 6–8 servings.

RASPBERRY BAVARIAN CREAM   HALLONFROMAGE

2 cups raspberries or 2 pack-	**1 envelope unflavored gelatin**
ages frozen raspberries	**¹/₄ cup cold water**
1 teaspoon lemon juice	**1 cup heavy cream, whipped**
½ cup sugar	

If you use frozen raspberries, use 1 package for the recipe, the second as
a sauce for the dessert.

Crush raspberries or place in electric blender; strain through a fine sieve.

Add lemon juice and sugar, and stir until sugar is dissolved.

Soften gelatin in cold water and heat until dissolved; add to raspberry
mixture and stir until blended; chill until mixture begins to thicken (about
20 minutes).

Fold in whipped cream.

Pour into 1 quart mold rinsed with cold water; chill in refrigerator until set

Unmold and serve garnished with additional raspberries and a few green
leaves.

Makes 4–5 servings.

MELON WITH RED
RASPBERRY PURÉE

A wonderful dish, which can be served either as a dessert or as an appetizer. When I serve it as a dessert, I sometimes soak the melon slices in rum a few hours before the sauce is poured over.

1 melon weighing about 4 pounds
1 cup fresh raspberries or 1 package frozen
1/3 cup sugar
1 tablespoon lemon juice

Cut melon into halves. Remove seeds. Scoop out pieces or balls from edible portion. Place in serving bowl.

Rinse and pick over raspberries. Place in a sieve over a small bowl and force raspberries through sieve, to remove seeds.

Add sugar and lemon juice to raspberry purée. (If frozen berries are used, omit sugar.)

Pour raspberry purée over melon; chill for several hours.

Serve fruit directly from bowl or pour into fruit cups.

Makes 4 servings.

QUICK AND EASY
BLUEBERRY DESSERT

RÅRÖRD BLÅBÄRSKRÄM

Very nice to serve on hot summer days. Remember it also when you have somebody sick in the house.

2 cups fresh blueberries
1–1 1/4 cups sugar (amount depends upon sweetness of berries)
1 tablespoon lemon juice
1 envelope unflavored gelatin
1 cup cold water

Rinse blueberries under cold water and place in large mixing bowl. Add sugar and lemon juice, and beat on lowest speed until sugar has melted.

Soften gelatin in cold water, heat until dissolved and add to berry-mixture.

Check seasoning once more for sweetness.

Pour mixture into a 1 quart bowl; chill for several hours.

Serve plain or with milk or cream.

Makes 4 servings.

FAVORITE BANANA DESSERT

BANANEFTERRÄTT
FAVORIT

If you like bananas, do not fail to try this recipe. It is luscious and easy to prepare.

6 large bananas
$1/2$ cup sugar
3 tablespoons lemon juice
$1/4$ cup egg whites (about 2 whites)   *Garnish:*
1 cup heavy cream, whipped $1/4$ cup chopped nuts
$1/2$ teaspoon vanilla   6 maraschino cherries

Peel bananas; mash and mix with $1/4$ cup of sugar and lemon juice.

Beat egg whites until stiff. Add gradually remaining sugar and beat until meringue holds stiff, but moist peaks.

Fold meringue into banana mixture and carefully blend in whipped cream and vanilla.

Spoon mixture into fruit cups or into a 6 cup serving dish. Garnish with chopped nuts and maraschino cherries. Chill.

Makes 6 servings.

STEWED RHUBARB

RABARBERKRÄM

1 cup water
1 cup sugar
3 cups cut-up fresh rhubarb
2 teaspoons corn starch
1 tablespoon water

Bring water and sugar to the boiling point. Add rhubarb and boil gently about 5 minutes or until rhubarb is tender. Taste to see if it's sweet enough. Add more sugar if necessary. Remove rhubarb with slotted spoon to serving dish.

Mix corn starch and water. Stir into syrup and bring to the boiling point, stirring constantly. Cook over low heat 3–4 minutes, or until clear. Stir occasionally. Pour over rhubarb. Cover and cool.

Serve with cream or milk.

Makes 4 servings.

151

Strawberry Parfait
Jordgubbsparfait

STRAWBERRY PARFAIT   JORDGUBBSPARFAIT

For a special Sunday dessert, whip up this smooth and refreshing ice cream.

$1/2$ cup sugar
$1/4$ cup water
2 egg yolks
$11/2$ cups fresh or frozen strawberries
2 teaspoons lemon juice
1 cup heavy cream, whipped

Mix sugar (if frozen strawberries are used, take only $1/3$ cup sugar) and water. Bring to the boiling point, simmer for 5 minutes.

152

Beat egg yolks in top of double boiler; gradually stir in sugar syrup.
Cook, stirring constantly over hot, not boiling water until thickened.
Remove from heat and continue to beat until mixture has cooled.
Crush strawberries well, remove $1/2$ cup for garnish. Stir remaining part
into egg yolk mixture, add lemon juice and whipped cream.

Pour mixture into one refrigerator tray, place in freezer compartment
and freeze until firm. If you remove tray from freezer 10 minutes before
serving time, the consistency will be much more creamy.

Turn parfait onto cold serving plate, cut into slices and spoon remaining
crushed strawberries over top. Garnish, if so desired, with some green leaves
and some additional whole strawberries, see picture beside.

Or, if you want to serve dessert out of parfait glasses, spoon layers of
parfait, crushed strawberries and whipped cream into glasses.

A heavenly dessert, but dangerous for plump waistlines.

Makes 4–5 servings.

STRAWBERRY
BAVARIAN CREAM

JORDGUBBSFROMAGE

1 quart hulled strawberries

1 cup sugar

2 envelopes unflavored gelatin

4 tablespoons cold water

1 tablespoon lemon juice

2 cups heavy cream, whipped

Put aside about 16 of the prettiest berries.

Crush the rest and add sugar. Let stand in room temperature for 15
minutes, stirring occasionally until sugar is dissolved.

Soften gelatin in cold water and heat until dissolved. Add to strawberry
mixture and stir in lemon juice. Chill mixture until it begins to set about
30 minutes.

Fold in whipped cream.

Rinse a 2 quart mold in cold water, spoon in strawberry mixture.

Chill several hours or until set.

Unmold, garnish with strawberries.

Makes 8 luscious servings.

FRUITS IN JELLIED WINE

A refreshing dessert, good after a substantial meal.

1 package lemon-flavored gelatin	1/2 pound seedless grapes
1 cup boiling water	3 large, ripe pears
1 1/2 cups white wine or sauterne	2 bananas
1/4 cup sherry or dry vermouth	

Place gelatin in a mixing bowl, add water and stir until dissolved. Cool. Add wine and sherry. Chill in refrigerator until it has consistency of unbeaten egg whites.

In the meantime prepare fruits. Separate grapes, peel pears and slice thinly (keep covered so they do not darken), peel bananas and slice lengthwise.

Rinse a 1 1/2 quart shallow bowl, or a pretty mold, with cold water.

Spoon in 1/4 cup of the partially set wine mixture, swirl bowl around to coat inside.

Place rows of grapes and banana slices in bottom of mold, or place fruits in any attractive pattern. Spoon over more gelatin mixture; chill until almost set. Fill bowl with layers of fruits. Spoon remaining gelatin mixture over (if too firm, melt slightly over heat). Chill until set.

Unmold by dipping bowl quickly in hot water.

Garnish with alternate clusters of blue and green grapes. If you desire a more filling dessert, serve with Uncooked Vanilla Sauce, see page 168.

Makes 6 servings.

MERINGUE PYRAMID
WITH CHOCOLATE SAUCE

Meringue:

3 egg whites
1/2 teaspoon cream of tartar
1 cup sugar
1 teaspoon vinegar
1/2 teaspoon vanilla

1 quart vanilla ice cream

Chocolate Sauce, see recipe, page 167

20 toasted, slivered almonds

Combine egg whites with the cream of tartar. Beat until soft peaks form. Add sugar a little at a time. Beat well after each time to dissolve sugar.

Add vinegar and vanilla and continue beating to stiff-peak stage

Cover two cookie sheets with heavy paper, draw 12 cup sized circles on one, 12 smaller circles on the other,

Spread meringue thinly in each circle. Make small peaks from remaining meringue.

Bake in a slow oven (300°) 20 minutes; then at 250° 15 minutes more.

Turn off heat, leave meringues in oven to dry. Lift gently from paper with a spatula.

Arrange a bottom layer with some of the large meringues on a platter. Spread a layer of ice cream on top, and continue to build up a pyramid of alternate layers of meringues and ice cream. Use the small meringues to make the top.

Dripple chocolate sauce from the top down and serve remaining sauce separately. Sprinkle with toasted, almond slivers. Serve immediately.

Makes 8–10 servings.

FUDGE PUDDING   CHOKLADPUDDING

For chocolate-lovers, here is a simple but excellent dessert.

1 envelope unflavored gelatin	$1/2$ cup water
$1/4$ cup water	$1/4$ cup butter or margarine
3 squares unsweetened chocolate	3 eggs, separated
$3/4$ cup sugar	1 cup heavy cream

Soften gelatin in water, place over hot water until dissolved.

Place chocolate, sugar and water in top of double boiler, leave until melted: stir in gelatin.

Drop in butter or margarine and beat until smooth, remove from heat.

Add egg yolks, one at a time, beating briskly.

Beat egg whites until they form stiff, but moist peaks.

Fold carefully into chocolate mixture.

Pour into a pretty 1 quart mold, brushed with oil or into an 8-inch pie plate; chill until set.

Whip cream and serve separately if a mold is used, otherwise spread over top of pie and serve in wedges. (If you want to make a graham-cracker pie shell, it will make the dessert still nicer.)

Makes 6 servings.

155

Chocolate Chiffon Pudding
Chokladfromage

CHOCOLATE CHIFFON PUDDING   CHOKLADFROMAGE

1 envelope unflavored gelatin
1/4 cup cold water
2 eggs, separated
1/2 cup sugar
3/4 cup milk

3 tablespoons cocoa
1/3 cup semi-sweet chocolate chips
1 teaspoon instant coffee
1 cup heavy cream, whipped
1 teaspoon vanilla

Soften gelatin in cold water.

Beat egg yolks with sugar until foamy.

Combine milk, cocoa and chocolate chips in saucepan. Cover and simmer until chocolate chips are melted. Pour mixture over egg yolks, a little at a time, stirring well. Return to saucepan. Add instant coffee and let mixture come to the boiling point, stirring constantly. Add gelatin and set pan in cold water. Stir occasionally until mixture starts thickening.

Beat egg whites until stiff; fold into gelatin mixture. Fold in whipped cream. Add vanilla.

Pour mixture into a 1 quart mold that has been rinsed with cold water or into individual molds. Chill until firm.

Unmold, garnish with peaches, whipped cream, maraschino cherries and cookies, see picture beside
Makes 6 servings.

RICE RING RIS À LA MALTA

This dessert is frequently served in Europe with a nice tart fruit sauce.

1/2 cup rice	3 envelopes unflavored gelatin
1 1/2 quarts boiling water	1/2 cup cold water
1 quart milk	1 pint heavy cream
3/4 cup sugar	1 tablespoon vanilla
1 teaspoon salt	1 tablespoon grated lemon rind
1 tablespoon butter	

Pour rice into boiling water. Boil briskly 2 minutes. Drain in sieve, rinse with cold water.

Return to pan. Add 2 cups milk, 1 tablespoon sugar, and salt. Bring to the boiling point; add butter. Cover, simmer 20 minutes, do not stir.

Pour into bowl. Add remaining milk and sugar. Cool.

Soften gelatin in cold water for 5 minutes. Heat slowly until gelatin dissolves. Add to rice. Chill until so thick that kernels don't sink.

Whip cream, adding vanilla and lemon rind gradually, as you whip. Fold into rice.

Pour into oiled, 2 quart mold. Cover with foil. Chill over night.

Serve with Cherry Sauce, see page 169.

Makes 8–10 servings.

RICE PUDDING RISGRYNSKAKA

Prepare Swedish Christmas Porridge, see page 61, and stir in 2 beaten eggs and 1 cup raisins.

Pour into buttered 6 cup baking dish.

Sprinkle with 1 tablespoon fine, dry bread crumbs; dot with 1 tablespoon butter or margarine.

Bake in hot oven (400°) 25 minutes or until set and golden brown.

Serve Rice Pudding hot or cold, with Fruit Syrup Sauce, see page 168, or Cherry Sauce, see page 169, or with jam.

Makes 6 servings.

Caramel Chiffon Pudding
Nougatpudding

CARAMEL CHIFFON PUDDING

NOUGATPUDDING

Caramel strips:

1¹/₂ cups sugar

¹/₂ cup chopped blanched almonds

Melt sugar in a grease-free frying pan over low heat. (Stir with table knife until melted.)

Add chopped and blanched almonds.

Stir until mixture starts to bubble, and has an amber color.

Pour onto *well-buttered* cookie sheet; mark six strips with knife dipped in oil to keep it from getting sticky.

Working very fast (before caramel gets hard), cut strips with oiled scissors, and shape over a jar.

158

Crush the rest of caramel into small bits and use as flavoring in

Cream Pudding:

2 envelopes gelatin
1/4 cup cold water
4 eggs separated
1/4 cup sugar
2/3 cup milk or cream

1 teaspoon vanilla
1 1/2 teaspoons grated orange rind
1 tablespoon rum or Swedish
   Punsch
1 tablespoon sugar
1 cup heavy cream, whipped

Soften gelatin in cold water.

Beat egg yolks with sugar until foamy.

Scald milk or cream and stir into egg mixture until blended.

Cook, stirring until thickened, in top of double boiler.

Add the softened gelatin, vanilla, orange rind and rum or Swedish punsch.
Cool, stirring occasionally until syrupy.

Beat egg whites until stiff, add gradually 1 tablespoon of sugar.

Fold whipped cream, egg whites, and crushed caramel into egg mixture.

Turn into 1 1/2 quart mold brushed with oil; chill until firm.

Unmold, place grapes or other fruits in groups alternatively with caramel
strips around pudding as garnish, see picture beside.

Makes about 6–8 very good servings.

CARAMEL CUSTARD   BRYLÉPUDDING

3/4 cup sugar
3 tablespoons boiling water
4 eggs
1/4 teaspoon salt
1 tablespoon vanilla

2 tablespoons sugar
1 cup milk
1 1/2 cups cream
   slivered almonds

Melt the 3/4 cup sugar in a heavy, grease-free, skillet – keep the heat low.
Stir occasionally with a metal knife until sugar is completely melted and
free of lumps. Add boiling water and cook until mixture is the consistency
of syrup.

Pour syrup into an 8-inch cake pan, turning pan constantly to coat sides
and bottom well. To make this easier heat cake pan a little before pouring
in syrup – it will run more freely.

Caramel Custard
Brylépudding

Break eggs into a large mixing bowl. Add salt, vanilla and sugar. Beat with rotary beater or electric mixer until frothy. Add milk and cream and beat again until thoroughly mixed.

Pour egg mixture into syrup-coated pan. Set pan in a larger baking pan and place in a slow baking oven (300°). Carefully pour hot water into pan until the level of the water is about $1/_2$ inch below rim of custard pan. Bake until a silver knife comes out clean when inserted in middle of custard; about 1 hour. Remove custard at once, lifting from water carefully; cool on cake rack.

Unmold on serving platter and garnish with slivered almonds, see picture above. Chill thoroughly before serving.

If you have trouble unmolding custard, set pan in hot water for a few moments to loosen caramel; or if you've baked it in a metal pan, set pan over low heat for a few moments.

Makes 6 servings.

MIXED FRUIT SOUP

BLANDAD FRUKTSOPPA

Many Americans like this typical Swedish Fruit Soup, which in Sweden is served chilled, for dessert. In America I have been served the same soup as salad with roasted pork which was also a nice combination.

2/3 cup dried apricots
2/3 cup dried prunes
6 cups water
1 stick cinnamon
2 lemon slices

2 tablespoons quick cooking
   tapioca
1/4 cup sugar
2 tablespoons raisins
1 apple, peeled and sliced

Wash dried fruits and soak in cold water half an hour.

Add cinnamon stick, lemon slices, tapioca and sugar; simmer covered until almost tender (about 10 minutes), stirring occasionally.

Stir in raisins and apple slices and cook a few minutes longer.

Taste soup, if you wish a stronger flavor add more sugar or lemon juice, or add 2 tablespoons of fruit syrup or grape juice.

Makes 4–5 servings.

POOR KNIGHTS (FRENCH TOAST)

FATTIGA RIDDARE

2 eggs
1 cup milk
1/3 cup cream
1 tablespoon sugar
1 teaspoon cinnamon or grated
   lemon peel

8 slices stale coffee bread or
   white bread
3 tablespoons butter or
   margarine, melted

Beat eggs with milk. Mix in cream, sugar, and cinnamon or lemon peel.

Soak both sides of bread slices in milk mixture for a few minutes. Fry in melted butter until nicely brown on both sides.

Serve very hot with jam or lingonberries.

Makes 4 servings.

Sauces

LEMON SAUCE (FOR FISH)   CITRONSÅS

3 tablespoons butter or margarine
1 tablespoon all-purpose flour
1/2 cup fish stock
2 egg yolks

1/2 cup cream
1-2 tablespoons lemon juice
1/2 teaspoon salt

Melt 2 tablespoons of the butter or margarine in saucepan. Stir in flour. Gradually add fish stock, stirring constantly; simmer for a few minutes.

Beat egg yolks with cream. Add to sauce gradually, stirring constantly, until sauce is smooth and thick. Remove from heat. Add lemon juice to taste, salt and remaining butter or margarine.

Makes 6 servings.

HORSERADISH SAUCE (FOR FISH)   PEPPARROTSSÅS

2 tablespoons butter or margarine

3 tablespoons all-purpose flour

2 cups milk and fish stock

1 teaspoon salt

1/8 teaspoon pepper

2-3 tablespoons grated horseradish, fresh or bottled

Melt butter or margarine in saucepan. Blend in flour. Gradually stir in milk. Cook, stirring, until smooth and thickened. Add salt and pepper.

Just before serving, stir in horseradish. (If sauce is cooked after adding horseradish, the flavor will be bitter.)

Makes 6 servings.

WHITE SAUCE   MJÖLKSÅS

3 tablespoons butter or margarine

3 tablespoons all-purpose flour

2 1/2 cups milk, or mixture of milk and cream

salt

pepper

162

Melt butter or margarine in saucepan.
Remove from heat and stir in flour. Gradually stir in liquid. Stir and cook until smoothly thickened.
Season with salt and pepper.
Serve with Boiled "Lutfisk", see page 52.
Makes 4 servings.

SHARP SAUCE SKARPSÅS

1 hard-cooked egg	dash of pepper
1 raw egg yolk	2 teaspoons sugar
1 teaspoon dry mustard	1 tablespoon good vinegar
$1/4$ teaspoon salt	$1/2$ cup heavy cream

Cut egg into half and separate yolk from white.
Press egg yolk through sieve; mix in raw egg yolk and seasonings.
Whip cream and fold gradually into sauce.
This sauce is sometimes flavored with a little finely chopped fresh dill.
The sauce is served with fried fish dishes, with Chicken Aspic, see page 124, or with Mixed Salad, see page 82, instead of a salad sauce.
Makes 4 servings.

HORSERADISH SAUCE (FOR MEAT) PEPPARROTSSÅS

2 tablespoons butter or margarine
2 tablespoons all-purpose flour
1 cup beef stock
1 cup milk
2-3 tablespoons grated horseradish, fresh or bottled
$1/2$ teaspoon salt

Melt butter or margarine in saucepan. Stir in flour. Gradually stir in beef stock and milk.
Cook, stirring constantly, until smooth and thickened.
Remove from heat and stir in horseradish and salt.
Do not cook sauce after adding horseradish or the flavor will be bitter.
Makes 4 servings.

DILL SAUCE

DILLSÅS

2 tablespoons butter or margarine
2 tablespoons all-purpose flour
2 cups lamb stock
2 tablespoons chopped dill

1 tablespoon white vinegar
2 teaspoons sugar
$1/4$ teaspoon salt
1 egg yolk, beaten

Melt butter or margarine in saucepan. Blend in flour. Gradually stir in stock. Cook, stirring, until smooth and thick. Remove from heat and stir in dill, vinegar, sugar and salt. Quickly stir in beaten egg yolk and serve immediately.
Makes 4 servings.

MUSHROOM SAUCE

SVAMPSÅS

$1/4$ pound mushrooms
2 tablespoons butter or margarine
$1/2$ teaspoon salt
   dash of pepper

2 tablespoons all-purpose flour
2 cups cream and milk or chicken
   bouillon and cream
1 tablespoon sherry, optional

Wipe mushrooms clean with damp paper towel.
Slice or halve mushrooms lengthwise. Place in saucepan with butter or margarine, salt and pepper.
Cover and cook over low heat 5 minutes.
Blend in flour, gradually stir in liquid.
Stir and cook until smooth and thickened; add sherry, if used.
Makes 4 servings.

CLEAR TOMATO SAUCE

KLAR TOMATSÅS

2 cups consommé or 2 cups water
   and 2 bouillon cubes
4 tablespoons tomato paste
1 tablespoon corn starch
3 tablespoons water

$1/4$ teaspoon salt
   dash of pepper
3 tablespoons sherry or
   dry vermouth, optional

Simmer consommé or water and bouillon cubes and tomato paste for about 10 minutes, in a covered saucepan.

Dissolve corn starch in water; stir into hot mixture. Bring sauce to the boiling point, continue to cook, stirring for 3–4 minutes until sauce is clear and smooth; turn off heat.

Season with salt, pepper and wine.

Serve sauce with baked ham or Fresh Beef Tongue, see page 132.

The same sauce can also be used for soup – add 1 cup light cream and in a few minutes time you will have a delicate cream of tomato soup.

Makes 6 servings.

HOLLANDAISE SAUCE   HOLLANDÄSSÅS

Follow recipe carefully and you will have an excellent result.

$3/4$ cup butter or margarine (or half of each)
4 egg yolks
1 tablespoon lemon juice
   dash of white pepper
   dash of salt

If your butter or margarine comes in $^1/_4$-pound sticks, use $1^1/_2$ sticks, cut the whole stick in half. If it doesn't come in sticks, divide the $^3/_4$ cup butter into 3 parts.

Pour egg yolks into top of a double boiler, add one portion of the butter. Set over hot but not boiling water. Stir rapidly until butter is melted. Add the second portion of butter, stirring constantly. As mixture thickens and butter melts, add the third portion, stirring vigorously from bottom of the pan. Do not allow the water over which the sauce is cooking to boil (will curdle sauce).

When butter is melted and all is well mixed, remove saucepan from heat and continue beating for at least 2 minutes more, or until sauce starts to thicken and get creamy.

Add lemon juice and white pepper. Taste before adding salt – the butter sometimes contains enough salt for the sauce.

Replace saucepan over hot but not boiling water and cook, beating constantly until sauce is the consistency of mayonnaise. Remove from heat and serve immediately with fish or vegetables.

LOBSTER SAUCE

Crabmeat or cooked shrimp may be used instead of lobster in this rich sauce.
Wonderful with omelets or various fish dishes.

1 cup lobster meat or 1 5-ounce
   can lobster meat
2 tablespoons butter or margarine
2 tablespoons all-purpose flour

1 cup lobster juice and milk
1 cup cream
1 teaspoon salt
   dash of cayenne

Drain lobster but save the juice. Cut lobster meat into pieces.

Melt butter or margarine in saucepan and stir in flour. Gradually stir in lobster juice, milk and cream. Stir and cook until smooth. Remove from heat.

Add lobster meat and season with salt and cayenne.

Reheat over low heat, being careful not to boil lobster.

ONION SAUCE

1 tablespoon butter or margarine
1 cup chopped onions
2 tablespoons all-purpose flour
$2^1/_4$ cups milk
$1^1/_4$ teaspoons salt
   dash of sugar

Melt butter or margarine in heavy saucepan.

Add onions and cook slowly, stirring occasionally, until tender. Sprinkle with flour. Gradually stir in milk. Cook, stirring constantly, until smooth and thickened. Add salt and sugar.

Serve with Fried Pork, see page 116.

Makes 4 servings.

BACON SAUCE

1 tablespoon butter or margarine
$3/_4$ cup chopped onion (about 1
   medium size onion)
8 slices bacon

2 tablespoons all-purpose flour
$1^3/_4$ cups milk
1 tablespoon tomato catsup
   salt

Melt butter or margarine in skillet. Add onion and sauté until almost soft.
Chop bacon with scissors directly into pan. Mix with onion and cook until crisp (about 5-6 minutes).

Sprinkle flour over mixture in skillet. Gradually stir in milk and cook, stirring, until smooth. Season with catsup; add salt to taste.

Serve as a filling in Spinach Ring, see page 78.

Sweet Sauces

BUTTERSCOTCH SAUCE   KOLASÅS

1 cup cream
1/3 cup dark corn syrup
2 tablespoons butter or margarine
1 teaspoon vanilla

Combine ingredients, cook over low heat until thickened (20-30 minutes), stirring occasionally.

Serve warm over baked apple dishes.

Makes 4 servings.

CHOCOLATE SAUCE   CHOKLADSÅS

1/3 cup sugar
1/2 cup cocoa
1 tablespoon corn starch
1 1/2 cups water
2 tablespoons butter or margarine

Mix sugar, cocoa, corn starch and water in small saucepan.

Cook, stirring until smooth; add butter or margarine and stir until well blended.

Serve warm or cold with Meringue Pyramid, see page 154.

VANILLA SAUCE

1 cup cream
1/2 vanilla bean or 2 teaspoons vanilla extract
3 egg yolks
2 tablespoons sugar

Heat cream with vanilla bean, or add vanilla extract when sauce is cool. Beat egg yolks and sugar until thick and foamy. Add a little of the cream to egg mixture; gradually pour this mixture into remaining cream in saucepan, stirring constantly.

Simmer gently, stirring, until thickened being careful so sauce will not boil. Pour immediately into a mixing bowl. Remove vanilla bean and beat sauce until it has cooled off. Chill.

Serve very cold with various apple desserts and pies.

Makes 4 servings.

UNCOOKED VANILLA SAUCE   OKOKT VANILJSÅS

A luscious sauce, served ice cold with apple desserts or other suitable fruit dishes. Very easy to make.

1 cup heavy cream
3 egg yolks
2/3 cup sifted confectioners' sugar
3/4 teaspoon vanilla

Whip cream until stiff.

Beat egg yolks while slowly adding confectioners' sugar and vanilla, beat until light and foamy.

Fold in whipped cream and chill well before serving.

Makes 4-6 servings.

FRUIT SYRUP SAUCE   SAFTSÅS

3/4 cup fruit syrup
1 cup water
2 teaspoons lemon juice
1 tablespoon corn starch
2 tablespoons water

Bring syrup and water to the boiling point. Add lemon juice.
Mix corn starch with water. Stir into syrup and bring to the boiling point
again stirring constantly. Reduce heat to low and cook, stirring occasionally,
3–4 minutes, or until clear. Cover and cool.
Serve cool with Rice Pudding, see page 157.

FRESH FRUIT SAUCE   BÄRSÅS

1 cup fresh berries
$1/4$ cup sugar
$3/4$ cup water
1 tablespoon corn starch
2 tablespoons cold water

Combine berries, sugar and water in saucepan. Bring to the boiling point.
Dissolve corn starch in cold water; stir into sauce. Cook stirring for
3–4 minutes, or until clear and shiny.
Strain sauce using a fine sieve. Pour into container with a cover. Cool.
Serve with Rice Pudding, see page 157.

CHERRY SAUCE   KÖRSBÄRSSÅS

3 cups pitted sour cherries
1 cup water
1 tablespoon lemon juice
$2/3$ cup sugar
2 tablespoons corn starch
$1/4$ cup water
1 tablespoon butter

Bring pitted sour cherries, water, lemon juice and sugar to the boiling point.
Mix together corn starch and water. Stir into sauce.
Cook, stirring, until thick and clear, 2–3 minutes. Remove from heat,
add butter.
(Sauce should be tart, but a little more sugar may be added if desired.)
Chill before serving.

169

The Best of
SWEDISH
BAKING

Yeast Breads, Coffeecakes and Danish Pastry

LIMPA BREAD

LIMPA

The limpa bread is typical of the northern part of Sweden. This recipe has found its way to many Swedish-American homes and has become very popular. The rye flor called for in this recipe is the fine kind which may be purchased in Swedish delicatesse stores. In Swedish it is named rågsikt.

2 tablespoons caraway seeds	2 packages of active dry yeast
1 tablespoon white vinegar	or compressed yeast
1$^1/_2$ cups lukewarm beer	2 tablespoons shortening
$^1/_4$ cup molasses	4 cups sifted rye flour
$^1/_4$ cup dark corn syrup	1$^3/_4$ cups sifted all-purpose
2 teaspoons salt	flour (about)

Place caraway seeds and white vinegar in a large mixing bowl together with beer, molasses, corn syrup and salt.

Sprinkle or crumble yeast into lukewarm liquid. Stir until dissolved, then add shortening.

Beat in rye flour first, then add all-purpose flour a little at a time. After you have added 1$^1/_2$ cups, turn the mixture out on floured board and knead for 10 minutes. Add remaining $^1/_4$ cup all-purpose flour if needed. Knead until dough is smooth and doesn't stick to the board.

Place the dough in a buttered bowl, turning the dough over so that it will be greased on all sides. Cover with a towel and let rise in a warm place (85°) until double in bulk. This will take about 2 hours.

To test if done: when the dough has doubled and is ready to be worked, press 2 fingers into it. If the indentations remain, the dough is ready.

Punch down, pulling the edges into the center, and turn dough over in the bowl. Let rise again until almost double in bulk (about 45 minutes).

Turn out on floured board and divide in 2 portions. Knead a few minutes. Shape into 2 loaves. Place on a buttered cookie sheet and let rise again until double in bulk 45–60 minutes. For the best textured bread, do not let loaves rise more than double at this point. Touch the loaf gently with a finger; if a slight indentation remains the loaves are ready for the oven.

Bake in a moderate oven (350°) for 30–40 minutes. To test for doneness: tap bottom of loaf; it should sound hollow.

This bread keeps very well.

RYE BREAD HÅLKAKOR

These have that real home-baked goodness in them. Eat bread while still warm, with plenty of butter and a slice of cheese.

1 package of active dry yeast
or compressed yeast
1/4 cup lukewarm water
1/4 cup shortening or lard
1 cup milk
1/3 cup dark corn syrup

1-2 teaspoons anise seeds
1 tablespoon grated orange rind
2 teaspoons salt
2 cups rye flour
1 1/4-1 1/2 cups sifted all-purpose
flour (about)

Sprinkle yeast in lukewarm water. Let stand 5-10 minutes until thoroughly dissolved.

Melt shortening or lard. Add milk and heat until lukewarm. Pour into big mixing bowl together with syrup, seeds, orange rind, salt, dissolved yeast and rye flour. Beat with wooden spoon until well blended. Gradually add 1 1/4 cups all-purpose flour. Beat dough until smooth and firm.

Flour board with remaining 1/4 cup all-purpose flour. Turn dough onto board and knead until smooth and elastic, about 10 minutes, using more flour if necessary.

Place dough in a buttered bowl. Turn dough over once to grease all sides. Cover, let rise in warm place until double in bulk, about 2 hours. When light, punch down, turn out on lightly floured board and knead dough for a few minutes.

Divide dough into 3 pieces. Shape each into round flat cakes about size of a saucer. Cut out a small hole in center. Place on buttered cookie sheet; brush with oil and prick with a fork dipped in flour. Cover and let rise, about 60 minutes.

Bake in moderate oven (375°) for 15-20 minutes or until light brown. To test if done: tap bottom of loaf; it should sound hollow. Remove to towels, brush with warm water and cover with towels.

Dough can also be shaped into 1 loaf. Prick with fork and let rise. Bake in moderate oven (350°) for 40 minutes, or until light brown. Brush with warm water when half-done and once again when baked.

GOOD COFFEE CAKE GOTT VETEBRÖD

This is a very Swedish kind of coffee cake which can be made into many different shapes of rolls, braided loaves and rings. It gets its distinctive flavoring from the cardamom seeds, added to the dough either in pounded or pulverized form. If you are especially fond of the way the Swedish coffee bread tastes, buy the whole seeds and crush them in a mortar or on a board with a rolling pin. It doesn't matter if the seeds are not completely crushed, they still give a wonderful aroma.

This type of coffee cake was formely baked in every Swedish home once a week and in such quantity that it lasted for a whole week; half of it was made into small coffee buns, half of it into braided loaves.

Many Swedish people, who have come to America, have told me they have tried to use their old Swedish recipe for baking this particular yeast dough, and have ended up with a hard inedible result, not taking into account how different American flour is. I can guarantee though that you will not end up like that with this recipe, which has been tested with American flour. It is a lot of fun to make and gives a splendid result.

2 packages of active dry yeast	$1/2$ teaspoon salt
or compressed yeast	$3/4$ cup scalded milk
$1/4$ cup warm water	1 egg
$2/3$ cup butter or margarine	$3^1/2$–4 cups sifted all-purpose
$1/3$ cup sugar	flour
2 teaspoons crushed cardamom	$3/4$ cup raisins, optional
seeds or 1 teaspoon pulverized	
ones	

Soften active dry yeast in warm water (110°); compressed yeast in luke-warm water (85°).

Mix together butter or margarine, sugar, cardamom, salt, and hot milk. Cool until lukewarm. Add egg, yeast and $2^1/_2$ cups of the flour. Beat thoroughly.

Add, a little at a time, enough of the remaining flour to make a soft dough, set a little aside for kneading.

Turn out dough on lightly floured surface, and knead until smooth and elastic, about 10 minutes. Place dough in a lightly buttered bowl, turn once to grease surface. Cover and let rise in warm place until doubled in bulk, about $1^1/_2$ hours. When light, punch down and turn out on lightly floured surface and knead lightly.

Form dough into various shapes, coffee cakes, braided loaves, cinnamon rings, cinnamon buns or into a birthday ring, as described in the following recipes.

Braided Coffee Loaves

Mix raisins with dough and divide into two or three parts, and cut each part into three pieces of equal size. Roll pieces into long ropes and braid three ropes together, making two or three braided loaves.

175

*Coffee Cake in two
different shapes*

Kaffekaka på två olika
sätt

*This is how we make
Cinnamon Buns*

Så här gör man kanel-
bullar

Shaping Cinnamon Ring

Hur man gör en kanel-
krans

Place on buttered cookie sheet; cover with towel and let rise in warm place until doubled in bulk (about 45 minutes).

Brush with beaten egg; sprinkle with sugar and chopped nuts, if so desired.

Bake in moderate oven (375°) 20–25 minutes. See color picture facing page 16.

Coffee Cake

Roll out dough into a rectangle about 24×10 inches. Spread surface with softened butter or margarine, sprinkle with sugar, raisins and chopped candied fruit if so desired. Roll dough lengthwise, as for jelly roll. Divide roll into 2 parts. Twist one and place it into a buttered, ring shaped mold to make a small ring. Cut through top part with floured scissors to make gashes about 2 inches apart, see picture, page 176. Cut the remaining roll into $1^1/_2$-inch thick slices, brush uncut sides with melted butter, and place pieces in a buttered round pan with cut side up. Let rise until almost doubled in bulk (about 1 hour).

Brush with beaten eggs, sugar and nuts.

Bake in moderate oven (375°) 25–30 minutes.

Cinnamon Buns

Roll out dough as for coffee cake. Spread rectangle with softened butter or margarine. Sprinkle with sugar and cinnamon. Roll up as for a jelly roll; cut roll into slices, or into different shapes, see picture, page 12. Place on buttered cookie sheet; cover and let rise until almost doubled in bulk (about 1 hour). Brush with beaten egg; sprinkle with sugar or nuts.

Bake in hot oven (400°) 6–8 minutes or until golden yellow.

See color picture facing page 191.

Cinnamon Ring

Prepare dough as above. Roll up and shape into ring on buttered cookie sheet. Leave whole or cut with scissors, see picture, p. 176, or as described for the birthday ring, see below.

Birthday Ring

Roll out dough into a rectangle 24 × 10 inches large.

Brush dough with 2 tablespoons melted butter; spread with filling, see next page.

Roll up dough lengthwise, as for a jelly roll. Shape roll into ring on buttered cookie sheet, around oven-proof container about 4 inches in diameter.

Cut through the ring diagonally with scissors. Then cut a diagonal slice $1/_2$-inch thick. Pull slice into petal shape, and flop it. Cut next two slices in same way and place them on either side of first slice, overlapping it a bit.

177

Repeat, cutting around the roll, forming a ring three petals wide.

Lightly press the outside edges of the finished ring with the palms of both hands, to make it compact and circular.

Let rise in warm place until doubled in bulk (about 40–60 minutes).

Bake in slow oven (325°) for about 30–35 minutes or until golden brown.

Allow to cool slightly before spreading with glaze, see below.

Filling:

1 egg white

1¼ teaspoons almond flavoring

²/₃ cup sugar

1 cup ground blanched almonds or other nuts

Beat egg white with a fork until slightly foamy.

Add almond flavoring. Gradually blend in sugar and nuts.

Glaze:

1¹/₂ cup confectioners' sugar

3 tablespoons water

¹/₄ cup sliced or chopped nuts

Mix sugar and water until smooth.

Spread over ring. Garnish with nuts.

If you bake the ring ahead of time, and freeze it, heat in a warm oven (250°) 10–15 minutes if ring is at room temperature, 25 minutes if ring comes direct from the freezer.

SAFFRON BREAD   SAFFRANSBRÖD

Saffron Bread is traditional for Swedish Christmas. It is strange, that this exotic spice, used so much in the rice dishes of the Orient, has found its way to this northern country. Here it is put into a sweet dough, which is shaped into very artistic looking buns, "lussekatter" in Swedish. See color picture facing page 16. These buns are served traditionally on the thirteenth of December, the day of St. Lucia, with the early morning coffee. Saffron gives the bread a lovely yellow color and a piquent flavor.

¹/₂ teaspoon saffron

1 cup lukewarm cream or milk

**2 packages of active dry yeast
  or compressed yeast**

¹/₃ cup sugar

¹/₂ teaspoon salt

1 egg, beaten

**¹/₂ cup butter or margarine,
  melted**

¹/₂ cup raisins

**4 cups sifted all-purpose flour
  (about)**

178

Dry saffron a few minutes in a very low oven temperature (otherwise it loses its color). Crush with mortar and pestle or with a spoon in a bowl until powdery. Spoon one tablespoon of warm cream or milk over saffron and let stand for a few minutes.

Dissolve yeast in remaining cream or milk; add sugar, salt, egg, butter or margarine, raisins, dissolved saffron and half of flour. Beat with wooden spoon until well blended, then gradually add more flour until dough is smooth and not too firm.

Turn dough out onto floured surface and knead for 10 minutes.

Place dough in a buttered bowl, turning the dough over so that it will be greased on all sides. Cover with towel and let rise in a warm place (85°) until double in bulk (about $1^1/_2$ hours).

Punch down dough. Knead dough lightly. Flour hands and shape the buns. Pinch off small pieces of dough and roll out on floured surface into 7-inch long strips. Pinch 2 strips together in the center; curl in each end. Stick a raisin in each curl; see upper right in color picture facing page 16.

This is the most common shape of these buns. You can also roll out thinner strips and place 3 together, so you will have 6 curls. Or you can just have one thick strip and roll ends into an S-shaped bun, see color picture facing page 16.

Place buns on buttered cookie sheet. Cover; let rise for about 45 minutes or until inpression remains, when finger is gently pressed into dough.

Brush buns with beaten egg.

Bake in hot oven (400°) 10–15 minutes.

Makes about 20 buns.

Dough can also be shaped into braided loaves or into a ring on a buttered cookie sheet. If you want it extra fancy, use a pair of scissors, and cut dough almost through into $1/_2$-inch slices, turning each back alternately to the right and to the left, see picture for Cinnamon Ring, page 176.

SHROVE TUESDAY BUNS   SEMLOR

Tradition is deep-rooted in Sweden, therefore many eating habits go back several generations. One of them is to serve the Shrove Tuesday Bun as dessert on the Tuesday night before Ash Wednesday and all through Lent. These buns are very popular and you will see them in many coffee shop windows in Sweden. They are rather large, light buns, sprinkled with confectioners' sugar and topped with whipped cream, see picture, p. 180. A generous slice of almond paste is inside the bun.

The buns are good, nourishing and lots of fun to prepare.

179

In Sweden Shrove Tuesday Buns are often eaten with hot milk and cinnamon
Semlor

1 package of active dry yeast
   or compressed yeast
$1/4$ cup warm water
1 egg
$2/3$ cup warm cream or milk
$1/4$ cup sugar
$1/4$ teaspoon salt

$1/2$ teaspoon cinnamon
$1/2$ cup soft butter or margarine
$3-3^1/4$ cups sifted all-purpose flour

Filling:
$1/4$ pound almond paste
$1/2$ cup heavy cream, whipped

Dissolve yeast in warm water.

Beat egg slightly and mix half of it with cream or milk and add to yeast; add sugar, salt, cinnamon, butter or margarine and part of flour. Add more flour a little at a time, beating with a wooden spoon to make a soft dough.

Turn dough unto floured board and knead until smooth and elastic (about 10 minutes). Place dough in lightly buttered bowl. Turn once to grease surface. Cover, let rise in a warm place (85°) until double in bulk about $1^1/_2$ hours. When light, punch down, turn out on floured board and knead lightly, until smooth. Shape into 10 round buns.

Place buns on buttered cookie sheet. Let rise in warm place until almost double in size. Brush with remaining egg.

Bake in hot oven (400°) until golden brown (10–12 minutes).
Cool on rack.

Cut off top slice from bun with sharp knife. Insert a slice of almond paste (see below) into bun, garnish with a generous tablespoon of whipped cream, replace top, and sprinkle with confectioners' sugar.

Serve in deep individual dishes with hot milk and cinnamon.

Makes 10 servings.

In case you are not able to buy almond paste, here is how to make it.

Almond Paste:

1/2 cup blanched almonds
1/2 teaspoon almond extract
1 cup sifted confectioners' sugar
1 egg white, slightly beaten

Put almonds through a nutgrinder or a food chopper, using fine blade. Place in a mixing bowl and sprinkle with almond extract and confectioners' sugar. Toss with a fork and gradually add egg white. Work paste until smooth. (Can be made ahead of time, wrapped in waxed paper and stored in room temperature in covered jar.)

DANISH PASTRY   DANSKA WIENERBRÖD

A delicious rich pastry, as good as any Danish pastry bought in Denmark or Sweden.

Butter dough:

1/3 cup sifted all-purpose flour
11/2 cups cold butter or margarine

Yeast dough:

2 packages of active dry yeast
  or compressed yeast
1/4 cup lukewarm water
1 cup cold milk   *Filling:*
1 egg, beaten   **choose from Almond Paste or**
1/4 cup sugar   **Vanilla Cream (see page 183)**
31/2 cups sifted all-purpose flour **or apple sauce**

181

Danish Pastry in different shapes (Crescents, Cockscombs and Envelopes)
Danska wienerbröd

Butter dough:
   Sift flour onto board. Cut butter or margarine into flour with 2 knives or pastry blender. Collect particles between floured hands and place on a piece of waxed paper; chill.

Yeast dough:
   Dissolve yeast in the lukewarm water.
   Add cold milk, egg and sugar; gradually add flour and beat with wooden spoon until smooth and glossy.
   Turn onto well floured surface and roll with floured rolling pin to a 14 × 14 inches square.
   Roll out butter dough to a 6 × 12 inches rectangle; it is easiest to do so, on a waxed paper and flip it on top of the yeast dough to one side of the square; fold plain half of dough over butter dough and press the edges together.
   Roll out into rectangle; having the long side of rectangle parallel with front edge of baking board and fold dough twice, from left to right, so you have 3 layers of dough.
   Turn dough a $1/_4$ of a turn to the right; roll out and fold twice again having the same size rectangle each time you roll out the dough; this rolling and folding is necessary to make the pastry flaky. Chill dough 1 hour.

182

To Shape Envelopes:

Roll out dough $1/4$-inch thick and cut it into 4-inch squares. Spread with 1 tablespoon filling. Fold corners into the center, pressing down edges firmly.

To Shape Cockscombs:

Roll out dough $1/8$-inch thick and cut it into long strips 5 inches wide. Place filling lengthwise down middle of strips, and fold both sides of dough over filling, so that you have 3 layers of dough. Coat with granulated sugar and chopped almonds. Cut in pieces 4 inches long and gash one side 5 times. Bend each one to separate gashes.

To shape Crescents:

Roll out dough $1/8$-inch thick and cut it into long strips 5 inches wide. Cut strips into triangles that are 3 inches wide at base. Place filling on base and roll up. Bend into crescent shapes.

Place all shapes on buttered cookie sheets; cover with clean towel and allow to rise in room temperature (not too warm) until almost doubled in bulk (about 1 hour). Brush Envelopes and Crescents with beaten egg. Bake in hot oven (425°) 12–15 minutes or until golden yellow. When cold, spread Envelopes and Crescents with icing made of 1 cup confectioners' sugar and 2 tablespoons water, stirred until smooth. See picture, p. 182.

Fillings, choose one of the two following kinds or use both.

Almond Paste:

$3/4$ cup unblanched almonds
$1/2$ cup sugar
1 egg, beaten
$1/2$ teaspoon almond extract

Grind almonds or chop finely and mix with sugar; gradually add egg and almond extract and work until smooth.

Vanilla Cream:

2 tablespoons sugar
1 tablespoon sifted all-purpose flour
1 egg yolk
$1/2$ cup milk
2 teaspoons vanilla extract

Mix sugar and flour in top of double boiler; mix in egg yolk and gradually stir in milk. Stir and cook over boiling water until thick. Cool, stirring occasionally; add vanilla.

FILLED COFFEE CRESCENTS NÖTGIFFLAR

These are delicate and easy to make. Serve with tea or coffee.

1 package of active dry yeast or
  compressed yeast
$1/4$ cup lukewarm water
2 cups sifted all-purpose flour
2 tablespoons sugar
$2/3$ cup butter or margarine
1 egg

Filling:

2 tablespoons butter or margarine
2 tablespoons sugar
$2/3$ cup chopped nuts

Garnish:

$1/2$ egg or 1 egg white

Soften yeast in lukewarm water.

Sift flour into bowl, add sugar; cut in butter or margarine with pastry blender or two knives until mixture resembles coarse corn meal. Stir in egg and dissolved yeast. Work dough with floured hands until smooth.

Cover; let rise 1 hour in room temperature.

In the meantime make the filling; cream butter or margarine with sugar and add chopped nuts.

Divide dough into 2 parts. Roll each part into a circle about 11 inches in diameter, cut each circle into 8 wedge shaped pieces. At wide end put 1 teaspoon of filling. Roll each piece by beginning at the wide end. (Stretch the wide end a bit as you start to roll it.)

Place rolls on buttered cookie sheet.

Brush rolls with $1/2$ beaten egg or 1 egg white. Permit rolls to rise in room temperature for about 1 hour or until an impression remains when finger is gently pressed into dough.

Bake in hot oven (400°) 8–10 minutes or until golden yellow.

Makes 16 crescents.

QUICK COFFEE CAKE KAFFEKAKA

This is an excellent coffee cake, not too sweet and very easy to make.

1 package of active dry yeast
  or compressed yeast
$1/4$ cup lukewarm water
$1/2$ cup cream or milk
1 egg, slightly beaten
2 cups sifted all-purpose flour

$1/4$ teaspoon salt
2 tablespoons sugar
$2/3$ cup butter or margarine
$3/4$ cup chopped citron or
  candied fruit or orange peel

184

Topping I:
2 tablespoons butter or margarine
1 tablespoon sugar

Topping II:
1 cup sifted confectioners' sugar
2 tablespoons orange juice

Sprinkle yeast in lukewarm water. Let stand until thoroughly dissolved.
Heat cream or milk until lukewarm, pour into mixing bowl and add egg.
Sift together flour, salt and sugar, add with yeast to cream. Beat until blended.
Cut in butter or margarine until mixture is lumpy, and not smooth.
Add chopped candied fruit, stir until ingredients are blended, not more.
Turn into a well buttered 9-inch square layer cake pan and spread with Topping I, dotting surface with butter or margarine and sprinkling with sugar.
Let rise in warm place (about 85°) until double in bulk, about 1 hour.
Bake in moderate oven (375°) for 20 minutes or until golden brown.
Cool coffee cake in pan, then remove and spread with Topping II (stir confectioners' sugar with orange juice until well blended).
Cut cake into square pieces and serve with tea or coffee.

CARDAMOM COFFEE CAKE   KARDEMUMMAKAKA

1 egg
1^1/$_4$ cups sugar
2 teaspoons whole cardamom seeds
^{3}/$_4$ cup milk
2^1/$_2$ cups sifted all-purpose flour
2^1/$_2$ teaspoons baking powder

^{1}/$_2$ teaspoon salt
1 cup butter or margarine, melted
Topping:
1 teaspoon cinnamon
1 tablespoon sugar
2 tablespoons chopped nuts

Beat egg until fluffy.
Add sugar gradually and stir until blended.
Crush cardamom seeds with a rolling pin or pound in a mortar with a pestle. Remove white hulls. Add cardamom to the egg-sugar mixture.
Heat milk until lukewarm and pour into the egg mixture alternately with the sifted dry ingredients.
Add melted butter or margarine and beat batter until well blended.
Butter a 9-inch square cake pan and sprinkle with 1 tablespoon dry bread crumbs. Shake off excess crumbs.
Pour batter into pan. Sprinkle cinnamon, sugar and nuts on top. Bake cake in moderate oven (350°) 35–40 minutes or until done.

185

COFFEE RING WITH SAFFRON

If you don't care for saffron, omit it and you will have a delicious biscuit ring.

2/3 cup butter or margarine
1/4 cup sugar
1/2 egg, beaten
1/2 teaspoon crushed cardamom
2 tablespoons chopped raisins
2 tablespoons chopped citron
1/2 teaspoon saffron, optional
1 teaspoon sugar

3/4 cup milk
2 1/2 cups sifted all-purpose flour
2 1/2 teaspoons baking powder

Topping:
1/2 egg, beaten
1 tablespoon sugar
2 tablespoons chopped nuts or
   almonds

Cream butter or margarine, gradually add sugar and cream together until light and fluffy.

Stir in egg, cardamom, raisins and citron.

If you use saffron, place it in a piece of foil, dry in slow oven a few minutes. Crush with 1 teaspoon sugar and dissolve in 1 tablespoon milk.

Sift together flour and baking powder.

Mix in flour, alternately with milk and stir until well blended.

Spoon batter on buttered cookie sheet into shape of a ring.

Brush ring with egg; sprinkle with sugar and nuts.

Bake saffron ring in slow oven (325°) for about 30–40 minutes or until golden brown.

FLUFFY WAFFLES

Good, inexpensive waffles to serve for sunday night suppers.

2 eggs, separated
1 1/2 cups milk
2 cups sifted cake flour
4 teaspoons baking powder

3 tablespoons sugar
1/4 teaspoon salt
6 tablespoons melted butter
   or margarine

Beat egg yolks until light; add milk.

Sift together flour, baking powder, sugar and salt and add to milk mixture.

Stir in butter or margarine.

Beat egg whites until they hold stiff, but moist peaks. Fold into flour mixture.

Bake in preheated waffle baker.

Makes 6 servings.

Cakes, Tortes, Pastries

SUNDAY CAKE SOCKERKAKSTÅRTA

A well known, often served cake in Sweden, which can be varied in many ways. If you are giving a big party, it is a good cake to serve; it keeps moist several days and is quite filling. See color picture facing page 207.

4 eggs
1 cup butter or margarine
2 cups sugar
3 cups sifted cake flour
3 teaspoons baking powder
1 cup milk
$1^1/_2$ teaspoons vanilla extract or grated lemon rind

Filling:
1 16-ounce package frozen strawberries
1 package vanilla pudding

Garnish:
$1^1/_2$ cups heavy cream, whipped
gum drops, candy wafers or fresh berries

Beat eggs until thick and lemon-colored.

Cream butter or margarine; gradually add sugar and continue to cream until very fluffy, then add beaten eggs a little at a time.

Sift flour with baking powder 3 times.

Add dry ingredients alternately with milk and vanilla or lemon rind, folding carefully until well blended.

Butter 2 9-inch round cake pans and sprinkle inside with 2 tablespoons fine, dry bread crumbs or until evenly coated. Pour batter into pans.

Bake in moderate oven (350°) 30–40 minutes or until done.

Remove from pans and cool.

Cut each layer in half, so that you will have 4 layers; fill and garnish.

Keep in refrigerator.

Makes 10–12 servings.

Filling:

Defrost strawberries. Cook vanilla pudding as directed on the package and cool.

Spread strawberries and vanilla pudding between layers of cake and cover with half of the whipped cream. Force remaining whipped cream through a pastry tube in a criss-cross pattern over cake and decorate with candy wafers, gum drops or fresh berries.

187

MOTHER'S FUDGE CAKE MORS CHOKLADTÅRTA

You will not be able to eat too big a piece of this rich, delicious fudge cake, but you will love every bit of it.

It keeps beautifully and can be served with different toppings – a sprinkling of confectioners' sugar, sweetened whipped cream sprinkled with a shaved chocolate bar, or with a chocolate icing.

$3/4$ cup blanched almonds or pecans

4 1-ounce squares unsweetened
  chocolate

$2/3$ cup butter or margarine

$2/3$ cup sugar

1 teaspoon vanilla extract

3 eggs, separated

$3/4$ cup sifted all-purpose flour

$1/2$ teaspoon baking powder

$1/4$ cup top milk or cream

Put almonds or pecans through a food chopper, or place in electric blender.

Melt chocolate over hot (not boiling) water.

Cream butter or margarine and sugar until smooth. Stir in ground nuts and vanilla. Pour in melted chocolate and beat for 5 to 10 minutes at high speed.

Add egg yolks one at a time, beating well after each yolk.

Sift flour with baking powder.

Mix half the flour into batter. Stir in milk or cream. Add remaining flour and mix until smooth.

Beat egg whites until they hold stiff but moist peaks; gently fold into batter.

Butter a 9-inch cake pan, sprinkle with 1 tablespoon fine, dry bread crumbs until evenly coated – shake off excess crumbs.

Spoon batter into pan and bake in moderate oven (325°) 30–35 minutes or until cake tester inserted in center of cake comes out clean. Cool cake in the pan for 10 minutes, then invert on cake rack.

Frost with sweetened whipped cream – use 1 cup heavy cream and $1^1/_2$ tablespoons sugar; or sprinkle cake with confectioners' sugar; or spread with Creamy Chocolate Frosting, see page 214.

CHOCOLATE CAKE CHOKLADKAKA

1 cup shortening

$1^1/_2$ cups sugar

3 eggs

2 squares unsweetened chocolate,
  melted

2 cups sifted cake flour

2 teaspoons baking powder

1 teaspoon salt

$1/4$ teaspoon baking soda

1 cup cream

2 teaspoons vanilla extract

188

Cream shortening. Add sugar gradually, creaming well.

Stir in eggs, one at a time, beating well after each addition.

Add chocolate.

Sift together dry ingredients.

Combine cream and vanilla. Add alternately with dry ingredients to creamed mixture, beginning and ending with dry ingredients. Blend thoroughly after each addition.

Butter a 10 × 4-inch round tube pan and sprinkle with 2 tablespoons dry bread crumbs until inside of pan is well coated.

Pour batter into pan and bake in slow oven (325°) for 50 – 60 minutes. Cool cake a few minutes before removing from pan.

Sift confectioners' sugar over cake when cool, or frost with Quick Chocolate Frosting, see page 214.

EXCELLENT CHOCOLATE
LAYER CAKE   FÖDELSEDAGSTÅRTA

Our favorite birthday cake.

4 1-ounce squares semi-sweet baking chocolate

$1/2$ cup boiling water

1 cup shortening

2 cups sugar

4 eggs, separated

1 teaspoon vanilla extract

$2^1/2$ cups sifted cake flour

1 teaspoon baking soda

$1/2$ teaspoon salt

1 cup buttermilk

Snowy White Frosting:

2 cups sugar

1 cup water

$1/8$ teaspoon salt

1 teaspoon white vinegar

3 egg whites

1 teaspoon vanilla extract

grated cocoanut or chopped nuts

Melt chocolate in the boiling water.

Cream shortening and sugar until light and fluffy.

Add egg yolks one at the time and beat well after each addition.

Add vanilla extract and melted chocolate and mix until blended.

Sift flour with baking soda and salt.

Add sifted dry ingredients alternately with buttermilk to butter and sugar mixture, beating after each addition until batter is smooth.

Beat egg whites until stiff and fold into cake batter.

Pour batter into three 8- or 9-inch layer pans, well buttered and dusted with dry bread crumbs.

189

Bake in moderate oven (350°) 35–40 minutes or until done. Cool.

Frost between layers, on top and sides. Top with grated cocoanut or chopped nuts.

Makes 8–10 servings.

Frosting:

Cook sugar, water, salt and vinegar in heavy saucepan over medium heat, stirring until clear. Then, without stirring, cook until mixture, at about 240°, forms a thin thread when dropped from a spoon.

Beat egg whites in large mixing bowl until stiff. Add hot syrup in a thin stream, beating constantly until frosting holds its shape. Add vanilla extract.

DREAM CAKE   DRÖMTÅRTA

Try this cake and you will understand why it is called "Dream Cake".

3 eggs

$2/3$ cup sugar   *Butter Cream Filling:*

$1/4$ teaspoon salt $1/4$ cup butter

$11/2$ teaspoons baking powder   1 egg yolk

4 tablespoons corn starch   1 teaspoon vanilla extract

2 tablespoons cocoa $3/4$ cup confectioners' sugar

Beat eggs in large mixing bowl until foamy; gradually add sugar and continue to beat 10–15 minutes or until very thick and foamy.

Sift together salt, baking powder, corn starch and cocoa twice.

Sift dry ingredients over egg mixture and fold in carefully.

Pour batter into a $15^1/_2 \times 10^1/_2 \times 1$-inch jelly roll pan that has been lined with buttered waxed paper.

Bake for 8–10 minutes in hot oven (400°). Be careful not to overbake. When a thin knife inserted in the center of cake, comes out clean, cake is done.

Remove cake from oven and loosen it from pan.

Turn out cake on a piece of waxed paper, sprinkled with granulated sugar, leaving the pan on top of cake to keep it moist. Let cool 20–30 minutes.

Remove pan and waxed paper.

Spread with Butter Cream Filling or Dream Filling, see recipes next page, and roll cake lengthwise into a long roll, see color picture facing p. 191.

Christmas Ginger Snaps, Braided Coffee Loaf, Spice Cake, Saffron Bread, Christmas Crullers, Grandmother's Jelly Cookies, Brandy Rings, Almond Tarts

To roll this delicate cake, lift up two corners of the waxed paper on which cake is resting and flip over about 2 inches of the cake onto itself. Continue to roll by lifting the waxed paper. The last flip should deposit the cake on a long wooden board or platter. Dust top with confectioners' sugar.
Makes about 15–18 slices.

Butter Cream Filling:
Cream butter, add egg yolk and vanilla. Beat in sugar gradually.

Dream Filling:
$3/4$ cup sweet butter
1 egg yolk
$1/4$ cup cocoa
3 cups confectioners' sugar
3 tablespoons rum

Cream butter with egg yolk and cocoa. Beat in sugar gradually, alternating with rum. Mix until smooth. Keep in room temperature.

JELLY ROLL WITH CHOCOLATE FILLING

RULLTÅRTA MED CHOKLADFYLLNING

This is one of the most popular cakes in Sweden. It makes a delightful dessert, served in thick slices with a scoop of vanilla ice cream. It is quickly made. If you do not like chocolate filling, use half a cup of red currant jelly.

4 eggs	*Chocolate Filling:*
$3/4$ cup sugar	$1/4$ cup butter
$3/4$ cup sifted cake flour	$3/4$ cup confectioners' sugar
1 teaspoon baking powder	1 egg yolk
1 teaspoon vanilla extract	1 teaspoon vanilla extract
2 tablespoons butter or margarine	$1/4$ cup cocoa

Beat eggs with sugar on high speed (10–15 minutes) until very thick and foamy.
Sift flour with baking powder; fold into egg mixture.
Add vanilla and melted butter or margarine and mix carefully.
Butter generously a jelly roll pan $15^1/_2 \times 10^1/_2 \times 1$-inch. Pour batter into pan; bake in hot oven (425°) for 8–10 minutes. When a thin knife inserted in center of cake comes out clean, cake is done.
Remove cake from oven and loosen it from pan.

Cinnamon Buns, Dream Cake, Jelly Roll; in the jars
Almond Tarts, Walnut Meringues and Almond Ginger Snaps

Turn out cake on a piece of waxed paper, sprinkled with granulated sugar, leaving the pan on top of cake to keep it moist. Let cool 20–30 minutes.

Remove pan and spread with Chocolate Filling or jelly. Roll cake lengthwise into a long roll, see color picture facing page 191.

To roll up this delicate cake, lift up two corners of the waxed paper on which cake is resting, and flip over about 2 inches of the cake onto itself. Continue to roll by lifting the waxed paper. The last flip should deposit the cake on a long wooden board or platter. Dust top with confectioners' sugar.

Makes about 15 slices of cake.

Is best to eat the same day, but keeps well in refrigerator rolled in waxed paper.

Filling:

Cream butter, add remaining ingredients and mix well.

JELLY ROLL WITH STRAWBERRIES AND WHIPPED CREAM

RULLTÅRTA MED JORDGUBBAR OCH GRÄDDE

A quickly made, light dessert, which looks quite elegant.

Make one Jelly Roll Cake, see Jelly Roll with Chocolate Filling, page 191. Fill with the following:

Strawberry and Whipped Cream Filling:

3 cups hulled strawberries

1/3 cup sugar

2 cups heavy cream, whipped

Save about half a cup of the nicest strawberries for garnish.

Chop the remaining amount very coarsely, add sugar and stir gently until dissolved. (Be careful not to make strawberries mushy, or the filling will be too loose.)

Remove one cup of whipped cream and save for garnish, fold remaining part into strawberry mixture.

Spread filling on cool cake and roll lengthwise.

Cover cake with whipped cream and garnish with strawberries and a few green leaves, see picture, next page.

Chill before serving.

Makes 10 servings.

Jelly Roll with Strawberries and Whipped Cream
Rulltårta med jordgubbar och grädde

MAZARIN CAKE

This is one of the most luscious cakes I know. It makes a marvelous dessert after a light luncheon, especially when served slightly warm.

Pastry:
1/2 cup butter or margarine
3 tablespoons sugar
1 egg yolk
1 cup plus 1 tablespoon sifted
  all-purpose flour

Filling:
1/3 cup butter or margarine
1/2 cup sugar
3/4 cup blanched almonds

1 teaspoon almond extract
5–6 drops green food coloring,
  optional
2 eggs
1 teaspoon all-purpose flour

Icing:
1 cup sifted confectioners' sugar
2 tablespoons boiled milk
1 tablespoon butter, melted
1 teaspoon vanilla

193

Pastry:

Cream butter or margarine with sugar.

Blend in egg yolk and flour; work until smooth. Shape pastry into a ball between lightly-floured hands. Chill well.

Place pastry between 2 pieces of lightly-floured waxed paper. Roll out to a circle about 11 inches in diameter. Lift off one piece of waxed paper and flip pastry into a buttered 8-inch pie plate. Remove other piece of waxed paper and, with floured hands, pat pastry firmly into pan so that all air bubbles are removed. Roll out remaining pastry into thin strips.

Filling:

Cream butter or margarine with sugar until fluffy.

Put almonds through a nutgrinder or food chopper using fine blade. Add almonds, almond extract and food coloring to creamed mixture. Add eggs, one at a time, blending well after each, and flour.

Or place all ingredients in an electric blender and mix until nuts are very finely chopped: turning off motor and scraping down sides often.

Spread filling over pastry. Protect pie edge with strips of aluminum foil. Place pastry strips over filling.

Bake in a slow oven (325°) until filling is set, about 35–45 minutes. Cool slightly in pan before spreading with icing.

Serve cake preferably the same day.

Makes 6 servings.

Icing:

Combine all ingredients and mix until smooth. Spread over cake, or if you would rather not ice the cake, just sprinkle with confectioners' sugar.

Mazarins (Mazariner):

Proceed as above, but bake in small buttered muffin pans in moderate oven (350°) for about 15 minutes. Top with confectioners' sugar or icing.

Makes 16 servings.

OPERA CAKE   OPERATÅRTA

This is a cake very often found in Sweden's many pastry shops. It has a light consistency and is quite delicate.

In Sweden it is always served coated with light green almond paste. For those who have no time to prepare the almond paste, I would suggest serving the cake plain with just the filling between the layers and on top. If you serve it very cold so the cream filling is almost frozen, the cake is at its best. Since the custard cream freezes very quickly, keep cake in refrigerator until dinner time, and place in freezer half an hour before serving.

3 tablespoons sifted all-purpose
 flour
3 tablespoons corn starch
$1/2$ teaspoon baking powder
$1/4$ teaspoon salt
4 eggs, separated
$2/3$ cup sugar

Custard Cream Filling:
$11/2$ teaspoons unflavored gelatin
2 tablespoons cold water
2 egg yolks

3 tablespoons sugar
1 tablespoon corn starch
1 cup milk
1 tablespoon vanilla extract
1 cup heavy cream, whipped
2 tablespoons Cointreau, optional

Almond Paste:
1 cup blanched almonds
$2/3$ cup confectioners' sugar
$11/2$ teaspoons almond extract
1 egg white
green food coloring

Sift together all-purpose flour, corn starch, baking powder and salt.
Pour egg yolks in bowl; add sugar and beat until white and fluffy.
Stir in flour mixture.
Beat egg whites until they hold stiff peaks; fold in carefully.
Pour batter into deep round cake pan which has been well-buttered and coated with fine, dry bread crumbs, or bake in 2 8-inch cake pans.
Bake in slow oven (325°) about 12–15 minutes or until done.
Cool cake.
Cut cake in 3 layers. Put cake together with Custard Cream Filling between the layers and on top of cake, cover with Almond Paste and sprinkle with confectioners' sugar. Keep in refrigerator until serving time.
Makes 6–8 servings.

Custard Cream Filling:
Soften gelatin in cold water.
Mix egg yolks, sugar, corn starch and milk in double boiler, stir and cook over simmering water until smooth and thick.
Remove from heat, add gelatin and vanilla and stir until gelatin is dissolved; stir occasionally until cold. Fold in whipped cream and Cointreau.

Almond Paste:
Put almonds through nut grinder twice. Work with sugar, almond extract and egg white until smooth, adding the desired amount green coloring and more confectioners' sugar, if needed. Roll out on waxed paper dusted with confectioners' sugar; shape into a large circle.

NUT FEATHER CAKE NÖTKAKA

A rich moist cake that will keep fresh for a long time if stored in a refrigerator.

2 eggs

1¹/₃ cups sugar

¹/₂ teaspoon almond extract

¹/₂ teaspoon salt

1¹/₂ cups sifted all-purpose flour

2 teaspoons baking powder

³/₄ cup filberts or hazelnuts

¹/₂ cup top milk or cream

²/₃ cup butter or margarine,
 melted

Beat eggs a few minutes; gradually add sugar and almond extract and continue to beat on high speed for about 10 minutes or until thick and foamy.

Sift together salt, flour and baking powder.

Grind nuts through a nut grinder. Mix with flour mixture on a piece of waxed paper.

Heat milk to lukewarm, stir milk and flour mixture alternately into batter. Pour melted butter or margarine into batter and stir until well blended.

Spoon batter into a buttered 10 × 5 × 3-inch loaf pan or 9 × 3¹/₂-inch tube pan, which has been coated with 1 tablespoon fine, dry bread crumbs.

Bake cake in slow oven (325°) for about 45–50 minutes or until done.

Allow cake to cool a few minutes in the pan before inverting on a serving plate. Sprinkle with confectioners' sugar or ice with Creamy Chocolate Frosting, see page 214. See color picture facing page 206.

TOSCA CAKE TOSCAKAKA

This is one of the best cake recipes from Sweden. My friends in America used to call it Almond Pie, which might give you an idea of how the cake will look.

2 eggs

1 cup sugar

1 teaspoon vanilla extract

1 cup and 1 tablespoon sifted
 all-purpose flour

1¹/₂ teaspoons baking powder

¹/₄ teaspoon salt

¹/₄ cup cream or top milk

¹/₂ cup butter or margarine,
 melted

Almond Sugar Topping:

¹/₃ cup almonds

¹/₄ cup butter or margarine

3 tablespoons sugar

2 teaspoons cream

1 tablespoon all-purpose flour

Beat eggs, sugar and vanilla extract together until light and fluffy.

Sift flour with baking powder and salt. Stir in flour mixture alternately with cream, stir until well blended.

Tosca Cake
Toscakaka

Add melted butter or margarine, blend until smooth.

Butter a 9-inch pie plate and sprinkle with fine, dry bread crumbs (about 1 tablespoon); coat well. Spoon batter into pan.

Bake in a slow oven (325°) for 30 minutes or until the middle of cake is firm. Remove cake from oven. Spread top very gently with Almond Sugar Topping (see below), see picture above. Turn up heat to 375°, return cake to oven and bake 5–10 minutes longer with a cookie sheet under the pan to prevent the bottom of cake getting overdone. Bake cake until topping is brown and bubbly.

Serve warm in wedges. Makes 6–8 servings.

Topping:

Blanch almonds. Remove skins and slice. (Almonds slice most easily if put in oven for about 5 minutes. Spread them out on a cookie sheet. Return to oven to reheat if they cool before you get them all sliced.)

Combine almonds with remaining ingredients in a small saucepan. Heat, stirring, until mixture begins to bubble. Remove from heat and stir briskly a few times.

197

SWEDISH FRUIT CAKE   SULTANKAKA

This Fruit Cake is not as sweet and rich as the American kind but it is much easier to make.

It is the kind of cake one never gets tired of. It keeps for months in the refrigerator.

1 cup currants or seedless raisins	1 cup butter (half margarine)
1¹/₂ cups candied mixed fruits	1 cup sugar
1³/₄ cups sifted all-purpose flour	3 eggs, separated
¹/₂ teaspoon baking powder	¹/₄ teaspoon cream of tartar

Rinse currants or raisins in cold water. Place in saucepan, cover with water. Let water come to the boiling point. Drain fruit. Dry thoroughly in towel.

Chop candied fruit or slice thinly (keep cherries whole). Mix fruits thoroughly with 1 cup of flour until coated.

Sift remaining flour with baking powder.

Cream butter; gradually add sugar and cream until white and fluffy.

Add one egg yolk at a time, beating well after each addition. Stir in floured fruit mixture and sifted ingredients. Mix thoroughly.

Beat egg whites a few minutes. Add cream of tartar and continue to beat until they form moist peaks. Fold in egg whites very carefully.

Butter a 9¹/₂ × 5¹/₄ × 2³/₄-inch loaf pan and sprinkle with fine, dry bread crumbs until evenly coated, shake off any excess.

Pour batter into loaf pan. Bake in slow oven (300°) for about 1¹/₂–2 hours, or until done.

Cool cake a few minutes before removing from pan.

This cake will keep moist for many months, wrapped in aluminium foil and stored in refrigerator. Do not cut cake before it is 2 or 3 days old.

LUSCIOUS POUND CAKE   GOD SOCKERKAKA

1 cup butter or margarine	3 cups sifted cake flour
2 cups sugar	¹/₂ teaspoon baking powder
4 eggs	¹/₂ teaspoon baking soda
2 teaspoons grated lemon rind	1 cup buttermilk
1 tablespoon lemon juice	

Cream butter or margarine with sugar until very fluffy.

Beat in eggs, one at a time: beat at medium speed until well mixed and add flavorings.

Sift dry ingredients together, add to egg mixture alternately with butter-milk. Beat until smooth on low speed.

Butter a 10×4-inch round cake pan or a 10×5×3-inch loaf pan. Sprinkle inside with 1 tablespoon dry bread crumbs, shake off excess crumbs.

Spoon batter into prepared pan and bake cake in slow oven (325°) for 1 hour and 15 minutes or until a tester comes out dry when inserted in the middle of the cake.

Cool cake and sift with confectioners' sugar before cutting.

SPICE CAKE   MJUK PEPPARKAKA

This is an excellent cake – moist, spicy and rich; keeps well.

1/2 cup shortening	1 teaspoon crushed cardamom,
1 cup sugar	optional
3 eggs	1/2 teaspoon salt
2 teaspoons cinnamon	1 teaspoon baking soda
1 teaspoon ginger	1 1/3 cups sifted all-purpose flour
3/4 teaspoon cloves	1 cup sour cream

Cream shortening and sugar together until fluffy.

Add eggs, one at a time, beating well after each.

Sift spices with salt, baking soda and flour twice.

Add flour mixture to creamed mixture alternately with sour cream. Blend well.

Butter a fluted 9×3$^1/_2$-inch tube pan, or a 9$^1/_2$×5$^1/_4$×2$^3/_4$-inch loaf pan and sprinkle with fine, dry bread crumbs, until inside of pan is well coated.

Spoon batter into pan. Bake in slow oven (325°) for about 50 minutes or until done.

See color picture facing page 190.

SAND CAKE   SANDKAKA

This will be a favorite for those who love pound cake. It is very delicate and keeps well. The potato flour gives it a special "sandy" texture.

1 cup butter or margarine	3/4 cup sifted potato flour
3/4 cup sifted cake flour	3 eggs
1/4 teaspoon salt	3 tablespoons brandy or rum
3 teaspoons baking powder	1 teaspoon grated lemon rind
1 cup sugar	

Melt butter or margarine and cool.

Sift cake flour, salt and baking powder twice.

Cream melted and cooled butter. Add sugar gradually. Beat mixture a few minutes more after all sugar has been added. Then gradually add potato flour and cream mixture until white and fluffy.

Add eggs one at a time, beating well after each addition.

Mix in brandy or rum and lemon rind.

Add sifted dry ingredients a little at a time. Mix thoroughly.

Butter a $9 \times 3^1/_2$-inch tube pan and sprinkle with 1 tablespoon dry bread crumbs. Spoon batter into pan and bake in slow oven (325°) for 45–50 minutes or until done. Cool cake slightly before removing from pan.

Sift confectioners' sugar over cake before serving. Or if you prefer to frost the cake, spread with Quick Orange Frosting, see page 214.

LUSCIOUS MERINGUE CAKE HERRGÅRDSBRÖD

3/4 cup butter or margarine

11/2 cups confectioners' sugar

3 eggs, separated

2 teaspoons grated orange rind

13/4 cups sifted cake flour

11/2 teaspoons baking powder

Meringue Topping:

1/2 cup egg whites

1 cup sugar

1/2 teaspoon vanilla extract

1/4 cup chopped nuts

1/4 cup currants or raisins

Cream butter or margarine with sugar until light and fluffy.

Beat in one egg yolk at a time, add orange rind.

Sift dry ingredients together and add to creamed mixture; blend well.

Fold in stiffly beaten egg whites.

Butter a $13 \times 9^1/_2 \times 2$-inch oblong cake pan and sprinkle with fine, dry bread crumbs until evenly coated; shake off any excess.

Spoon batter into cake pan; bake in moderate oven (350°) 20–25 minutes or until center of cake is just firm. Spread with meringue and sprinkle with nuts and currants, see below.

Bake 5–10 minutes or until meringue is golden yellow. Cool cake slightly before cutting into squares. Serve preferably while still warm.

Topping:

Beat egg whites until they form soft peaks.

Add gradually sugar and vanilla and continue to beat until peaks hold stiff points.

OLD-FASHIONED SWEDISH SPONGE CAKE

This is in Sweden called Sockerkaka – Sugarcake – and there are hundreds of variations of this recipe.

This particular recipe is very old and, to my taste, it is an excellent one. It is light and golden. Although best the first day, it will keep well.

You will find it pictured in the Midsummer Coffee Party, facing page 33.

5 large eggs, separated	$1^1/_4$ teaspoons baking powder
1 teaspoon grated lemon rind	4 teaspoons corn starch
1 tablespoon lemon juice	1 cup sifted all-purpose flour
3 tablespoons water	minus 4 teaspoons of the flour
1 cup sugar	$1/_2$ teaspoon salt

Butter a fluted 10×4-inch tube pan, sprinkle inside with 2 tablespoons fine, dry bread crumbs, until evenly coated; shake off any excess.

Beat egg yolks, lemon rind – add juice and water on high speed until mixture has thickened.

Add sugar gradually, continue to beat until sugar is completely dissolved and mixture thick and light in color.

Sift baking powder, corn starch and flour together twice.

Fold in flour carefully until well blended.

Beat egg whites until foamy, add salt and continue to beat until egg whites hold stiff but moist peaks.

Fold in egg whites carefully until evenly blended. Spoon batter into prepared pan.

Bake in slow oven (325°) for about 50 minutes.

Let cool a few minutes in pan before unmolding.

When cool sprinkle with confectioners' sugar, or frost with Strawberry Frosting, see page 215, or Quick Orange Frosting, see page 214.

AMBROSIA CAKE

2 eggs	*Ambrosia Icing:*
$2/_3$ cup sugar	1 cup sifted confectioners' sugar
$2/_3$ cup butter or margarine	2 tablespoons concentrated orange
2 teaspoons grated orange rind	juice
$3/_4$ cup sifted cake flour	3 tablespoons candied orange peel,
$3/_4$ teaspoon baking powder	or sliced, toasted almonds
$1/_4$ teaspoon salt	

Beat eggs with sugar until light and fluffy.

Cream butter or margarine with orange rind.

Sift flour with baking powder and salt.

Add creamed butter to egg mixture alternately with sifted dry ingredients. Blend thoroughly.

Butter one 8-inch layer cake pan and sprinkle with fine, dry bread crumbs (about 1 tablespoon). Spoon batter into pan.

Bake in slow oven (325°) for about 25–30 minutes, or until done.

Cool cake in pan for 10 minutes, then remove from pan and cool slightly before spreading with icing.

Makes 6–8 servings.

Icing:

Mix sugar and orange juice until smooth. Spread over top and sides of cooled cake.

Cut orange peel into small squares and sprinkle over icing, or if almonds are used, sprinkle slices of almonds over icing.

WALNUT CAKE   VALNÖTSTÅRTA

Neither rich nor sweet, this cake makes a delicious dessert.

4 eggs, separated	*Filling:*
1/2 cup sugar	1 cup heavy cream, whipped
3 tablespoons corn starch	1–2 tablespoons rum, optional
1/2 teaspoon salt	(or Swedish Punsch)
1/2 teaspoon baking powder	1 tablespoon sugar
1 1/4 cups coarsely chopped walnuts	1/2 teaspoon vanilla extract
	2 tablespoons chopped walnuts

Beat egg yolks a few minutes.

Add sugar gradually and continue to beat on high speed until very thick and foamy (10–15 minutes).

Sift corn starch, salt and baking powder together. Stir flour mixture gradually into egg mixture.

Chop walnuts very fine or place in electric blender; add to batter.

Beat egg whites until they hold stiff, but moist peaks; fold gently into cake batter.

Butter 2 8-inch cake pans and sprinkle with 2 tablespoons fine, dry bread crumbs until coated.

Spoon batter into cake pans and bake in slow oven (325°) for about 20 minutes or until done. Cake can also be baked in a deep, 8-inch round cake pan and then cooled, cut into layers.

Spread filling between layers and sprinkle top of cake with confectioners' sugar. If desired, cake can also be spread with additional whipped cream and sprinkled with a coarsely grated chocolate bar.

Chill several hours before serving or place it in a freezer for $1/_2$ hour.

Makes 6–8 servings.

Filling:

Mix all ingredients gently until well blended.

FILLED CREAM PUFF RING

FYLLD PETITS-
CHOUX-KRANS

This is a truly delicious dessert, easy to make and yet very "fancy" looking. It looks like it comes out of a famous chef's kitchen. You can make it the day of your party or ahead of time and freeze it.

1 cup water

1/4 cup butter or margarine

1 cup sifted all-purpose flour

1/4 teaspoon salt

4 small eggs (break eggs into glass measuring cup, shall measure 6 oz.)

Filled Cream Puff Ring
Fylld petits-choux-krans

203

Put water and butter or margarine in saucepan, let come to the boiling point.

Remove pan from heat; add flour and salt, all at once, stirring constantly. Return to heat and cook until mixture leaves sides of pan in a smooth compact ball. Remove from heat and cool for about 1 minute.

Beat eggs slightly in the measuring cup and add gradually to cooked mixture, beating vigorously until mixture is smooth again.

Butter a cookie sheet and dust with flour. Trace around an 8-inch cake pan to make a circle. Spoon batter inside of circle to make a ring or use a pastry bag with a pastry tube inside.

Bake in hot oven (400°) for 30—40 minutes or until light and firm.

The cooled ring can be filled with ice cream, whipped cream mixed with fresh chopped strawberries, or Custard Cream Filling, see page 195.

Just before serving, cut off top of ring.

Spoon filling on bottom layer, put top over, sprinkle with confectioners' sugar or spread with Creamy Chocolate Frosting, see page 214, and top with chopped nuts. See picture, page 203.

Serve plain or with whipped cream.

Makes 8–10 servings.

THOUSAND LEAVES TORTE   TUSENBLADSTÅRTA

This torte has got its name because of the great flakiness of the pastry.

2 cups sifted all-purpose flour
1 cup butter or margarine
4–5 tablespoons ice water

Filling:
apple sauce (thick)
Custard Cream Filling, see
page 195

Icing:
1¹/₂ cups sifted confectioners'
sugar
1 tablespoon water
2 tablespoons lemon juice or cordial

Garnish:
1/₂ cup heavy cream, whipped,
optional
candied orange peel, cut in strips,
or toasted blanched almonds

Sift flour into mixing bowl. Cut in butter or margarine with pastry blender or 2 knives, until pieces are the size of peas. Add ice water gradually. Toss gently with fork. Gather up with fingers; form into ball. Chill ¹/₂ hour.

Divide dough into 6 portions. Roll each very thinly between 2 lightly-floured pieces of waxed paper. Remove top sheet of waxed paper. Cut out

Thousand Leaves Torte. It is easier to decorate top layer before placing it on torte
Tusenbladstårta. Det är lättare att garnera den översta bottnen innan man lägger
samman tårtan

circle and prick with fork. Place circle with waxed paper still underneath on
cookie sheet. Brush with water and sprinkle with sugar.

Bake in hot oven (425°) until golden brown, about 5–6 minutes.

Cool layers before removing paper.

Place the bottom layer on a round platter, then spread layers alternately
with Custard Cream Filling and apple sauce.

Garnish torte, if you like, with sweetened whipped cream, forced through
a pastry tube, and slices of candied orange peel or toasted, almond slivers.
Torte should be served immediately.

Makes 8–10 servings.

Icing:

Stir ingredients for icing together until of spreading consistency, and
spread over top layer.

OLGA'S ORANGE CAKE OLGAS APELSINKRANS

A perfect party treat without much preparation.

1 round orange chiffon cake
3 egg whites
1 6-ounce can concentrated orange juice
1 cup heavy cream
1 tablespoon sugar
grated cocoanut or chopped nuts

Buy cake at your local grocery store or make it from a cake mix. Cut cake into 3 layers.

Beat egg whites until stiff. Slowly add defrosted orange juice and continue to beat until smooth. Spread egg white mixture between layers and over cake. Let cake stand in refrigerator over night.

Beat heavy cream with sugar until of spreading consistency. Spread over cake.

Decorate cake with grated cocoanut or chopped nuts.

Keep in refrigerator until serving.

Serve plain or with fresh strawberries.

Serves 8—10.

DELICIOUS APPLE TORTE ÄPPLEFLARN

1¹/₂ cups sifted all-purpose flour	**5–6 apples**
2 teaspoons sugar	**2 tablespoons butter, melted**
1 cup butter or margarine	**1 tablespoon sugar**
4–5 tablespoons cream	**¹/₂ cup apricot jam, melted**

Mix flour and sugar together. Cut in butter or margarine. Gradually add cream, one tablespoon at the time or just enough to make particles stick together. Mix lightly with fork. Form into ball. Chill.

Roll out pastry on cookie sheet, about ¹/₄ inch thick. Place a 9-inch round cake pan on pastry, and cut around edge with a knife to get a round bottom crust. Bake crust in moderate oven (375°) 15 minutes.

Roll remaining pastry into a long strip 1¹/₂ inch wide. Peel and slice apples into thin wedges. Arrange apples in circles on the crust and tuck the pastry strip around the edge of the cake. Brush with melted butter and sprinkle with sugar.

206

Almond Lace Cookies, Meringue Torte with Strawberries, Nut Feather Cake with frosting, Almond Rings, Orange Nut Squares, Chocolate Brownies, Butter Leaves, Spritz Rings, Dream Cookies

ROYAL CHOCOLATE TORTE

Ever since I can remember, this torte was served on special occasions in my parents' house. It is a very unusual recipe – the layers are made from a cookie dough so that they are thin and crisp; and the filling is mellow and creamy.

For easier preparation, bake the layers a day ahead of time (keeping them crisp in an airtight container). Make the filling in the morning and put the torte together when filling is cold. It keeps beautifully for a long time, although the layers will not stay crisp, but many people prefer the torte that way.

Layers:
- 2 1/3 cups sifted all-purpose flour
- 1/2 teaspoon baking powder
- 1/2 cup sugar
- 1/2 cup cocoa
- 1 cup butter or margarine
- 1 egg yolk

Chocolate Filling:
- 2 egg yolks
- 1/3 cup sugar
- 3 tablespoons all-purpose flour
- 1 1-ounce square semi-sweet baking chocolate
- 1 cup light cream or top milk
- 3/4 cup heavy cream, whipped

Sift dry ingredients into large mixing bowl.
Cut in butter or margarine with pastry blender or 2 knives.
Add egg yolk; work pastry with your hands until smooth; chill.
Divide pastry into 3 parts to make 3 layers.
Roll each part between 2 sheets of lightly floured waxed paper to a 9-inch circle. Remove top sheet of waxed paper and flip that side down onto a buttered cookie sheet. Remove other sheet of waxed paper.
Bake for 12–15 minutes, or until firm, in moderate oven (375°). Be careful not to overbake layers, as that will make them bitter.
Loosen layers immediately with sharp knife, but leave on cookie sheets until cool. Remove carefully (easiest way is to slide a cardboard underneath).
To keep layers crisp avoid baking on a humid day.
Spread layers and top of torte with filling, but not sides.
Serve chilled.

Chocolate Filling:
Mix all ingredients in small saucepan except for heavy cream. Place over very low heat and let slowly come to the boiling point, while stirring constantly. Beat vigorously for another minute, or until completely smooth. Remove from heat and stir occasionally until cool.
Add whipped cream and stir gently until well blended.

Bake (with a second cookie sheet underneath, to keep
too brown) in moderate oven (350°) for 20 minutes.
Remove torte from oven and brush the apples with me
Continue to bake for 10 minutes or until golden color.
Serve slightly warm, plain or with whipped cream or ic
Serves 6—8.

MERINGUE TORTE WITH STRAWBERRIES

MARÄ
MED J

This is a really light torte, easy to prepare and delightful to

2/3 cup egg whites (about 4 eggs)
1 cup sugar
1/4 teaspoon almond extract
1/4 cup finely chopped walnuts

Filling:

1 1/2 cups heavy crear
2–4 tablespoons rum.
1–2 tablespoons suga
3 cups hulled strawber
2 tablespoons sugar

Cover 2 cookie sheets with brown paper. Draw two circles usin
cake pan as a guide. Oil paper, sprinkle lightly with flour.
Beat egg whites with hand- or electric beater until stiff enoug
in moist peaks, when beater is raised. Add sugar gradually, bea
ously. Add almond extract and beat until stiff and glossy. Fold in
mix until smooth.
Spoon half the meringue neatly into each circle (should be abou
thick). Bake in very slow oven (250°) for 1 hour, or until surface
when touched.
Loosen meringue from paper with a spatula and cool.
About half an hour before serving time, place one meringue lay
serving plate, cover with mashed strawberries and half the whipped
Place second layer on top, cover with whipped cream and garnis
whole strawberries, see color picture facing page 206. Place in freez
refrigerator) for half an hour, or until serving time.
Makes 6–8 servings.

Filling:

Flavor whipped cream with rum and sugar to suit your taste.
Reserve 1 cup of the prettiest strawberries for garnish. Lightly r
remaining strawberries with a fork – they should not be mushy – and spri
with sugar.

VIRGINIA TORTE

Despite its American name, this recipe is a modern Swedish Torte, extremely good and much in demand. It is easy to make if you follow instructions carefully. However it needs a bit of extra care while baking. The layers can be baked a day before the party, and stored in a tightly covered container. The cake can also be fully prepared and placed in freezer ahead of time. Remove 10 minutes before serving.

Same ingredients as Almond Lace Cookies, see page 223

2 cups heavy cream or
1¹/₂ quart ice cream or
Custard Cream Filling, see page 195

Make one batch of Almond Lace Cookies, see page 223.

Butter *very well* and *dust with flour* 3 cookie sheets (if you do not have so many, you have to repeat the baking after cookie sheet has cooled).

Divide cookie batch into 3 parts and spread out into a small circle on each cookie sheet.

Bake in moderate oven (375°) for 4 minutes or until cookie mixture has spread out. With a spatula shape nut mixture into about a 9-inch circel. Return to oven and bake 3–4 minutes longer or until golden brown. Remove cookie sheet and let cool about 2 minutes, before removing layer with *sharp, slender knife*. Transfer carefully to a double piece of waxed paper or cardboard. For easier handling, lift on waxed paper to serving plate or place in container for storage.

Fill with heavy cream, whipped and seasoned with vanilla or rum, with Custard Cream Filling, see recipe page 195, or with vanilla ice cream.

When using ice cream as filling, pour softened ice cream into 2 9-inch round cake pans lined with waxed paper and freeze. Unmold ice cream between layers, garnish top with dollops of whipped cream and a grated chocolate bar.

Serve with warm chocolate sauce.

Makes 8–10 delicious servings.

ALMOND TORTE "WITHOUT RIVAL"   SANS RIVAL

This is a very rich torte. You will find it in several variations on the continent. It is usually served in small squares. In Sweden this is regarded as our most delicious torte.

1 cup blanched almonds

2 cups sifted confectioners' sugar

5 egg whites

1/2 teaspoon cream of tartar

Butter Cream:

1 cup sweet butter

4 tablespoons water

1/3 cup granulated sugar

3 egg yolks

1 teaspoon vanilla extract

Praline:

1/2 cup granulated sugar

1/2 cup blanched almonds

Garnish:

20 toasted almonds

Grind almonds through a nut grinder. Mix with sugar.

Beat egg whites a few minutes. Add cream of tartar. Continue to beat until they form stiff peaks. Fold in almond mixture very carefully.

Butter 2 cookie sheets very well and sprinkle with flour. Measure out 3 8-inch squares on cookie sheets. Spread meringue into the squares. Bake in slow oven (300°) for about 18–20 minutes, or until light yellow in color.

Remove immediately from cookie sheet with sharp, thin knife. Layers get crisp as soon as they cool.

Spread butter cream between cool layers and cover top and sides. Garnish top with toasted almonds (cut into halves). Sprinkle sides with praline.

This torte keeps very well for several days, stored in refrigerator. Let torte stay at room temperature for about 1 hour before serving as a dessert.

Makes 8–10 servings.

Praline:

Melt sugar in skillet over low heat. Add whole almonds to syrup and pour out on a well-buttered cookie sheet. Let cool until very stiff.

Break praline into small pieces and grind these.

Add 2/3 of ground praline to butter cream and save the rest for garnish on torte.

Butter Cream:

Cream butter well. Boil water with sugar until syrup spins a 2-inch thread, when dropped from fork or spoon (230°). Beat egg yolks until blended. Pour a little at a time of the syrup over egg yolks, beating vigorously. When cream is smooth and cool, add butter very carefully, a little at a time (too much at a time will curdle butter cream). Add vanilla. If cream curdles, place bowl over pan with hot water and beat vigorously until smooth.

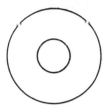

| *Christmas Star* | *Envelope* | *Butter Ring* |

How to shape Swedish Puff Paste
Utbakning av smörbakelser

SWEDISH PUFF PASTE SMÖRBAKELSER

2 cups sifted all-purpose flour
1 cup cold butter or margarine
4–5 tablespoons icewater

Measure flour into bowl.

Cut in butter or margarine with 2 knives or pastry blender until the pieces are the size of peas.

Add water gradually, toss lightly. Collect particles and shape into a round ball between floured hands. Handle dough as little as possible.

Chill dough for 30 minutes – makes it easier to handle.

Turn chilled dough onto floured board. Roll into a rectangle (12 × 7-inch) and $^1/_4$-inch thick.

Mark dough into 3 parts. Fold one third of the dough over the center part and the remaining third of the dough on top, making 3 layers. Turn dough over and roll out to rectangle again; repeat folding and rolling twice more. Chill for 30 minutes. Repeat once more folding and rolling as described above.

This folding and rolling makes the pastry extra flaky and tender but can be omitted if your time is short. Roll out dough into a thin rectangle.

To shape Christmas Stars (Julstjärnor):

Cut 4-inch squares. Place a teaspoon of jam in middle of each. Slit each corner $1^1/_2$ inches toward center; fold alternate points into center and press together, see sketch above. Brush with beaten egg and bake in hot oven (425°) 7–10 minutes, or until flaky and golden yellow. Eat slightly varm.

To shape Envelopes (Konvolut):

Cut 4-inch squares. Place a teaspoon of jam in middle of each. Fold 2 opposite corners in slightly, then fold to almost join in the center, see sketch above. Brush with beaten egg and bake as described above.

Makes 12 large pastries.

RASPBERRY FLARN

HALLONFLARN

Rich Pie Pastry:

1¹/₂ cups sifted all-purpose flour
4 teaspoons sugar
²/₃ cup butter or margarine
3–4 tablespoons water

Raspberry Filling:

1 cup sugar
2 tablespoons quick-cooking tapioca
³/₄ teaspoon cinnamon
3 cups firm raspberries, not too ripe
1 egg
2 tablespoons sugar

Sift flour and sugar together.

Cut butter or margarine into flour with pastry blender or 2 knives.

Sprinkle water, 1 tablespoon at a time, over mixture, tossing quickly with a fork until dough forms a ball. (Use only enough water to make flour particles cling together – they should not be wet or slippery.)

Form pastry into smooth ball between floured hands; chill well before rolling.

Roll on floured board into a 14 × 10-inch rectangle.

Roll pastry around floured rolling pin; transfer pastry carefully, so it will not stretch, to unbuttered jelly roll pan, or cookie sheet. A pan with sides will keep juice from running out.

Spread filling in center of pastry.

Bring sides up over filling, fitting points closely, and seal the ends. Pinch corners together.

Beat egg; brush over pastry, sprinkle with sugar.

Bake in moderate (375°) oven 25 minutes, or until golden yellow.

Let cool slightly before cutting.

Serve with ice cold whipped cream, or ice cream.

Makes 6 servings.

Filling:

Mix sugar, tapioca, and cinnamon; sprinkle over berries. Mix gently with forks so that berries will not be crushed.

GOOSEBERRY PIE

KRUSBÄRSPAJ

¹/₂ recipe of Rich Pie Pastry, see Raspberry Flarn above

Gooseberry Filling:

¹/₂ cup water
2 cups sugar – or less according to sweetness of berries
6 cups gooseberries
¹/₄ cup corn starch

Roll pastry very thin to make a 12-inch circle.

Place loosely in 10-inch pie plate, pat out any air bubbles. Avoid stretching the pastry, or it may shrink during baking.

Prick with fork dipped in flour, particularly around sides. Pinch overhang under the edge of pie plate to prevent sides from sliding down while baking.

Bake shell in moderate (375°) oven about 10–15 minutes; cool. You can prepare this shell a day ahead.

Fill pie shell.

If you wish, serve with whipped cream.

Makes 8 servings.

Filling:

Boil $^1/_4$ cup water and the sugar for a few minutes over low heat.

Cut off stem and blossom tips from berries. Add to syrup.

Simmer gently about 4 minutes, or until berries are cooked but still whole.

Using a slotted spoon, remove berries from syrup; cool. Place berries in pie shell.

Dissolve corn starch in remaining $^1/_4$ cup water. Stir into syrup.

Cook syrup until thick and clear, about 3 minutes, stirring constantly.

Cool to lukewarm. Pour over berries.

DEEP-DISH RHUBARB PIE   RABARBERPAJ

2 pounds young rhubarb stalks

1$^1/_2$ cups sugar

3 tablespoons all-purpose flour

1 tablespoon butter or margarine

1 recipe Rich Pie Pastry, see Raspberry Flarn, page 212

Cut unpeeled rhubarb stalks into 1-inch pieces (should measure 4 cups).

Mix rhubarb with sugar and flour and put mixture into a deep 8-inch pie dish or casserole, with a custard cup inverted in the center to prevent crust from sagging. Dot with butter or margarine.

Cover dish with Rich Pie Pastry. Press edges to the dish with tines of fork. Slash dough in several places for steam to escape. Roll out remaining dough, and cut out to leaves or long strips and garnish pie as you desire.

Bake pie in hot oven (450°) for 10 minutes. Reduce heat to 350° and continue to bake for 30 minutes longer, or until almost done.

Sprinkle crust with 1 tablespoon sugar and bake for another 10 minutes, or until sugar is melted.

Makes 6 servings.

Frostings

CREAMY CHOCOLATE FROSTING   CHOKLADGLASYR

1 package semi-sweet chocolate
  pieces
$1/2$ ounce square unsweetened
  chocolate
1 teaspoon butter or margarine

$1/3$ cup milk
1 teaspoon instant coffee
1 egg yolk
$3/4$ cup sifted confectioners' sugar

Blend chocolates, butter or margarine, milk and instant coffee in top of double boiler. Place over hot water until chocolate melts.
Remove from heat. Beat with spoon until smooth.
Stir in egg yolk, beating vigorously.
Add confectioners' sugar, and beat until cool enough to spread.

QUICK CHOCOLATE FROSTING   KOKT CHOKLADGLASYR

1 cup sugar
1 egg, beaten
2 tablespoons cream
2 squares unsweetened chocolate
3 tablespoons butter or margarine
1 teaspoon vanilla extract

Combine frosting ingredients. Bring to boil, stirring constantly. Remove from heat; stir until of spreading consistency.

QUICK ORANGE FROSTING   APELSINGLASYR

$1/4$ cup butter or margarine
1 egg yolk
3 cups sifted confectioners' sugar
1 tablespoon grated orange rind
3 tablespoons concentrated orange juice

Cream butter or margarine; gradually add remaining ingredients and stir until well blended.

214

CHOCOLATE ICING

2 1-ounce squares semi-sweet chocolate   2 tablespoons butter or margarine
1/3 cup cream   1 cup confectioners' sugar

Melt chocolate over hot water.

Add cream and butter or margarine, stirring vigorously until butter is melted. Remove from heat and beat in sugar. Continue to beat until smooth and of spreading consistency.

Spread over top and sides of torte and sprinkle top, if you wish, with a few chopped nuts.

STRAWBERRY FROSTING

JORDGUBBSGLASYR

1 cup sugar   2 egg whites
1/2 cup frozen strawberries, defrosted 1/4 teaspoon salt
1 tablespoon lemon juice   1/2 teaspoon cream of tartar

Place sugar, defrosted strawberries and lemon juice in small heavy saucepan. Cook mixture slowly over low heat, stirring occasionally, so that strawberries do not stick to the bottom.

Cook until mixture forms a thin thread, when dropped from a spoon (at about 230°). Remove from heat.

Beat egg whites with salt and cream of tartar until stiff.

Add hot syrup in a thin stream, beating constantly on high speed until frosting holds its shape.

SKILLET CHOCOLATE
MOCHA FROSTING

MOCKAGLASYR

1 cup sugar   1 1-ounze unsweetened baking
2 tablespoons evaporated milk   chocolate
1 egg, beaten   1 tablespoon instant coffee

Combine sugar, milk, egg and baking chocolate in skillet. Place over low heat. Bring mixture slowly to a boil, stirring constantly.

Remove from heat and stir in instant coffee.

Beat until foamy and of spreading consistency.

Makes enough to frost sides and top of a 8 inch layer cake.

Cookies

CHRISTMAS GINGER SNAPS   PEPPARKAKOR

*These cookies belong to the Swedish Christmas tradition and are a "must"
in every Swedish home.*

$2/3$ cup shortening

$3/4$ cup sifted light brown sugar,
   firmly packed

2 tablespoons molasses

3 tablespoons boiled, cooled water

1 teaspoon grated lemon rind

$2^1/4$ cups sifted all-purpose flour

1 teaspoon baking soda

1 tablespoon cinnamon

$1^1/2$ teaspoons cloves

1 teaspoon pulverized or ground
   cardamom seeds

Cream shortening and sugar thoroughly. Add molasses, water and lemon
rind.

Sift flour with baking soda and spices. Add to creamed mixture a little
at a time. Blend well.

Flour hands, toss dough quickly on floured surface and place in refrigerator; chill.

Turn dough onto floured surface. Roll out very thin and cut in desired
shapes with floured cookie cutters.

Bake on buttered cookie sheet in moderate oven (350°) for 8–10 minutes.
Cool cookies on sheet. Garnish if desired with Snow Icing, see Ginger Cookie
House, page 218. See color picture facing page 190, and black and white
picture, page 217.

Makes about 60 cookies.

GINGER COOKIE HOUSE   PEPPARKAKSHUS

*The ginger cookie dough that is used is slightly stiffer than ordinary dough –
so the cookie house won't crumble.*

1 cup shortening

1 cup brown sugar

1 tablespoon grated lemon rind

1 tablespoon cinnamon

1 tablespoon ginger

1 cup dark corn syrup

2 eggs, beaten

$5^1/2$–6 cups sifted all-purpose flour

$1/2$ teaspoon salt

$1^1/4$ teaspoons baking soda

Snow Icing:

1 pound confectioners' sugar

3 egg whites

1 tablespoon white vinegar

216

Christmas Ginger Snaps
Pepparkakor

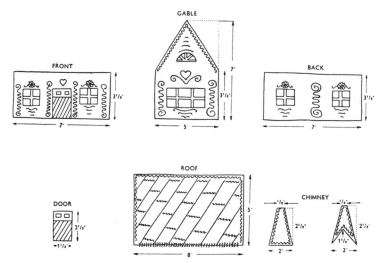

Pattern for Ginger Cookie House
Mönster till pepparkakshus

217

Ginger Cookie House
Pepparkakshus

Cream shortening; add brown sugar, lemon rind, and spices.

Bring syrup to a boil; pour into shortening mixture, stir until well blended. Add eggs and blend.

Sift 3 cups flour with salt and baking soda; add to mixture at once. Stir then in $2^{1}/_{2}$ cups flour, a little at a time.

Turn out on lightly floured surface and knead about 10 minutes, using remaining $^{1}/_{2}$ cup flour if necessary.

Chill for 1 hour.

Separate dough into several sections. Roll out to $^{1}/_{4}$-inch thickness. Transfer to buttered cookie sheet; smooth out dough with rolling pin. Dust patterns for house pieces (see drawings, page 217) with flour; place on dough and cut out with a sharp knife.

Bake in moderate oven (375°) 12–15 minutes for large pieces, 5–7 for the small pieces. Cool.

218

Sugar-syrup "glue" to make the house:

Melt 2 cups of granulated sugar in a heavy shallow skillet (at least 12-inches across); use lowest heat to melt sugar.

Stir constantly while sugar melts, so that it won't burn. Keep syrup on medium heat while you use it. Be sure to use a wide skillet, so that you can dip edges of long cookies into the syrup easily, as you put the house together.

Icing:

Place sugar in mixing bowl.

Beat egg whites slightly with fork.

Add to sugar and beat with electric mixer on lowest speed for one minute.

Add vinegar and beat 2 minutes more at high speed, or until stiff and glossy – as for stiff meringue.

Ice the house according to pictures on pp. 217 and 219, using a fine pastry tube, or spread icing all over the roof.

LARGE CRISP GINGER SNAPS   STORA PEPPARKAKOR

$3/4$ **cup shortening**

1 cup brown sugar

$1/4$ **cup light molasses**

1 beaten egg

$2^1/4$ **cups sifted all-purpose flour**

2 teaspoons ginger

$1^1/2$ **teaspoons cinnamon**

$1/2$ **teaspoon cloves**

2 teaspoons baking soda

$1/4$ **teaspoon salt**

25 blanched almonds

Cream shortening and sugar thoroughly. Add molasses and egg. Beat until well blended.

Sift dry ingredients. Add to creamed mixture. Mix well.

Roll dough into balls (about $1^1/2$ inches in diameter). Place $2^1/2$ inches apart on buttered cookie sheet. Flatten slightly and press an almond in each cookie.

Bake in moderate oven (350°) 12–15 minutes.

Makes 25 large cookies.

ALMOND
GINGER SNAPS

3¹/₃ cups sifted all-purpose flour

1¹/₂ teaspoons baking soda

3 teaspoons ginger

2 teaspoons cinnamon

2 teaspoons cloves

1 cup butter or margarine

1 cup sugar

¹/₂ cup dark corn syrup

1 cup blanched almonds, coarsely
  chopped

Sift together flour, baking soda and spices.

Cream butter or margarine; gradually add sugar; cream until fluffy.

Stir in corn syrup, almonds and flour mixture and blend thoroughly.

Turn onto lightly floured surface and knead until smooth.

Shape into 2 thick, long rolls or oblong shapes. Wrap each in waxed paper and chill thoroughly.

Cut with sharp knife into thin slices. Place on buttered cookie sheet.

Bake in moderate oven (350°) 8–10 minutes or until lightly browned. Leave on cookie sheet to cool.

Makes about 100 cookies.

SPRITZ RINGS

These cookies are so famous that in America they are often called Swedish Spritz.

1 cup butter or half butter substitute

¹/₂ cup sifted confectioners' sugar

1 egg yolk

1 teaspoon almond extract

¹/₃ cup blanched almonds, ground

2 cups sifted all-purpose flour

Cream butter and sugar very well. Add egg yolk and almond extract. Stir in ground almonds and flour a little at a time until dough is smooth and not too firm.

Shape with cookie press into rings or S's on buttered cookie sheet. Bake in moderate oven (375°) 8–10 minutes or until golden yellow. See color picture facing page 206. Let cookies cool on sheet.

Makes about 45 cookies.

SPRITZ COOKIES

ENKLA SPRITSAR

Very easy to make and a favorite in the cookie jur.

$^3/_4$ cup butter or margarine
1 cup light brown sugar, firmly packed
1 tablespoon vanilla extract
1 egg white
2 teaspoons milk
2 cups sifted all-purpose flour
a pinch of salt

Cream butter or margarine with brown sugar and vanilla until light and fluffy.
Add egg white and milk alternately with flour and salt; blend until smooth.
Force dough through cookie press onto buttered cookie sheets into bars about 3 inches long and $1^1/_4$ inches wide.
Bake in moderate oven (375°) 8—10 minutes or until golden brown.
Makes about 50 cookies.

COCOANUT SPRITZ COOKIES

KOKOSSPRITSAR

$^2/_3$ cup butter or margarine
$^2/_3$ cup sugar
1 cup fine-grated cocoanut
1 egg
$^1/_2$ teaspoon baking soda
$1^3/_4$ cups sifted all-purpose flour

Cream butter or margarine with sugar until light and fluffy.
Blend in cocoanut and egg, cream until smooth.
Sift baking soda with flour and stir into the batter.
Force through cookie press on buttered cookie sheets into rings, about 2 inches wide.
Bake cookies in moderate oven (350°) 8—10 minutes or until golden yellow.
Makes about 60 cookies.

221

ALMOND TARTS

MANDELFORMAR

³/₄ cup sweet butter
²/₃ cup sugar
1 cup blanched almonds

1 teaspoon almond extract
1 egg
2¹/₂–2²/₃ cups sifted all-purpose flour

Cream butter and sugar until light and fluffy.

Grind almonds in nutgrinder or in meatgrinder, using fine blade.

Add almonds, almond extract and egg and mix until well blended. Stir in 2¹/₂ cups of flour.

Remove dough from bowl and knead lightly on floured surface until smooth, using remaining flour if necessary. Chill well.

Butter very well insides of small fluted tart molds with *margarine or butter.* Using your thumbs, coat the insides evenly with a thin layer of dough, see picture above.

Bake in moderate oven (375°) 12–15 minutes or until light golden color. See color picture facing page 190.

Turn molds upside down and tap gently with a spoon to loosen tarts, or place a cold, wet towel over inverted molds. Lift molds from tarts and cool.

Serve plain or filled with whipped cream, topped with a spoonful of raspberry jam. Makes about 45 tarts.

ALMOND RUSKS MANDELSKORROR

1/3 cup butter or margarine	2/3 cup coarsely chopped almonds
3/4 cup sugar	or pecans
2 eggs	1 3/4 cups sifted all-purpose flour
3/4 teaspoon almond extract	1 1/2 teaspoons baking powder

Cream butter or margarine with sugar until light and fluffy.
Beat in eggs, almond extract and chopped almonds; mix until smooth.
Sift flour and baking powder together. Stir gradually into the batter.
Spread batter onto buttered cookie sheets into 1 1/2 inches wide strips.
Bake in moderate oven (375°) 8–10 minutes or until golden yellow.
Remove from oven and cut strips immediately into 1/2 inch wide slices.
Separate them so they lay flat on the cookie sheets.
Turn off oven heat and return cookies to dry slightly for about 15–20 minutes.
Makes about 45 rusks.

ALMOND LACE COOKIES MANDELFLARN

2/3 cup blanched almonds	3 teaspoons all-purpose flour
1/2 cup sugar	2 tablespoons light cream
1/2 cup butter or margarine	

Grind or chop almonds very fine or place in electric blender.
Mix almonds with remaining ingredients in heavy pan, place over low heat; stirring until butter melts. (Cook until bubbly and pulls away from side of pan as cream puff batter.)
Drop teaspoonfuls of mixture about 4 inches apart *on well buttered and floured cookie sheets.*
Bake in moderate oven (375°) until light brown 5–6 minutes. Let cool about 1 minute before removing cookies with *sharp, slender knife.* Leave cookies flat if you want so and place two together with a good butter cream between, see Chocolate Filling, page 191, or hang them over a clean broom handle to make curls, see picture of Oatmeal Wafers, page 241.
These cookies are extremely tender and lacy looking and have to be handled very carefully or they will break.
If cookies should be too crisp to remove from cookie sheet, return to oven for a few seconds. Don't try to do too many at a time.
These cookies are usually served with a molded dessert, like a Bavarian Cream, or with tea and coffee at festive occasions. See color picture facing page 206. Makes about 40 cookies.

ALMOND RINGS

20 chopped blanched almonds
1 cup butter or margarine
$1/3$ cup sugar
$1/3$ cup blanched almonds

$1/2$ teaspoon almond extract
2 egg yolks, beaten
$1^1/3$ cups sifted all-purpose flour

Butter small, fluted ring-shaped tins. Sprinkle with chopped almonds.
Cream butter or margarine with sugar until light and fluffy.

Grind almonds through a nut grinder or chop finely. Add remaining
ingredients to creamed mixture. Mix thoroughly.

Spread evenly in tins and bake in slow oven (325°) for 20 minutes or until
golden yellow. Allow to cool in tins before unmolding.

Sift confectioners' sugar over cold cookies. See color picture facing p. 206.
Makes 20 cookies.

WALNUT MERINGUES

Delicate and well flavored.

$2/3$ cup egg whites
$2^2/3$ cups sifted confectioners' sugar
$3/4$ cup chopped walnuts

Combine egg whites and sugar in top of double boiler. Put over hot, but
not boiling, water and beat vigorously with rotary beater or electric mixer
until very stiff peaks form. Fold in walnuts very carefully.

Drop by teaspoonfuls on well buttered and floured cookie sheets.

Bake in slow oven (300°) for about 25–35 minutes, or until light yellow,
see color picture facing page 207. Remove gently from cookie sheets with
sharp knife.

Makes about 60 meringues.

BRANDY RINGS

A recipe more than 100 years old; a favorite morsel through the generations.

$1^1/3$ cups butter
$3/4$ cup sugar
1 egg yolk
4 tablespoons brandy
$3^1/4$ cups sifted all-purpose flour

Cream butter with sugar until smooth and fluffy.

Beat in egg yolk and brandy. Blend in flour. Mix well. Chill dough thoroughly It should be quite cold for easy handling so we suggest you work with small portions of the dough at a time, keeping the rest in the refrigerator.

With floured hands, pinch off small pieces of dough and roll on lightly floured surface into thin lengths slightly thinner than a pencil and about 5 inches long. Make ropes by twisting two of these pieces together like twine. Shape each rope into a ring.

Bake on buttered cookie sheet in moderate oven (350°) until golden yellow, about 10–12 minutes, see color picture facing page 190.

Makes about 60 cookies.

UPPÅKRA COOKIES
UPPÅKRAKAKOR

1 cup butter
$1/2$ cup sifted confectioners' sugar
$1/2$ teaspoon vanilla extract
$2/3$ cup potato flour
$1^1/2$ cups sifted all-purpose flour

1 egg, slightly beaten
$1/3$ cup chopped almonds or pecans
3 tablespoons granulated sugar

Cream butter; gradually add sugar and cream until light and fluffy. Add vanilla, potato flour and all-purpose flour. Blend well. Chill dough for $1/2$ hour.

Pinch off a small piece of dough at a time, leaving the rest in the refrigerator.

Knead dough lightly between floured hands and roll $1/8$-inch thick between two pieces of waxed paper sprinkled with flour. Cut rounds with floured 2-inch cookie cutter; fold over almost in the middle. Use spatula or knife to lift cookies to buttered cookie sheet. Brush with egg. Mix chopped nuts and sugar together; sprinkle over cookies.

Bake in moderate oven (350°) until golden yellow, about 10 minutes.

Makes about 50 cookies.

FARMER'S COOKIES
BONDKAKOR

Easy to do and good for all occasions.

2 cups sifted all-purpose flour
1 teaspoon baking soda
1 cup butter or margarine
$3/4$ cup sugar

1 tablespoon dark corn syrup or
  molasses
$1/3$ cup finely chopped pecans.

Sift together flour and baking soda.

Cream butter or margarine and add gradually sugar, cream until light and fluffy.

Blend in corn syrup, chopped pecans and flour mixture a little at a time. Mix well.

Shape dough on lightly floured surface into long rolls about 2 inches in diameter. Wrap in waxed paper; chill.

Slice thinly with sharp knife. Place on buttered cookie sheets. Bake in moderate oven (350°) 10 minutes or until golden yellow.

Makes about 60 cookies.

CURRENT COOKIES KORINTKAKOR

2/3 cup currants
1 cup butter or margarine
1 cup sugar
1 egg, beaten
1 teaspoon vanilla extract
2 1/3 cups sifted all-purpose flour

Scald currants; dry on absorbent paper.

Cream butter or margarine; gradually add sugar and cream until fluffy. Add egg, vanilla, currants and flour, mix until smooth.

Chill dough in refrigerator for 1 hour. Pinch off small pieces and roll between floured. hands into 1-inch balls; place on buttered cookie sheet. Flatten them with a fork, dipped in flour.

Bake in moderate oven (350°) 8–10 minutes or until golden yellow.
Makes 60 cookies.

VANILLA COOKIES VANILJKAKOR

Tender and rich cookies, at their best when made from butter.

1 cup butter or margarine
1/2 cup confectioners' sugar
1 egg yolk
2 teaspoons vanilla extract
2 1/4 cups sifted all-purpose flour

Garnish:

1 tablespoon red currant jelly

226

Cream butter or margarine; gradually add sugar and cream until light and fluffy.

Beat in egg yolk, vanilla and flour; blend thoroughly.

Force dough through broad pastry tube onto buttered cookie sheet, forming large rosettes, or drop by spoonfuls onto buttered cookie sheet.

Put a little piece of jelly on top of each cookie.

Bake in moderate oven (350°) about 8 minutes or until golden yellow. Sift confectioners' sugar over cold cookies. See color picture facing p. 207. Make about 50 cookies.

DELICIOUS SHORTBREAD   MÖRA KAKOR

Very easy to make and a real treat.

1/2 cup butter	1/2 teaspoon vanilla extract
1/3 cup confectioners' sugar, firmly packed	1/4 cup cornstarch
	1 1/2 cups sifted all-purpose flour

Cream butter with confectioners' sugar and vanilla until light and fluffy.

Add cornstarch and flour: blend until smooth.

Drop by teaspoonfuls on buttered cookie sheets.

Bake in moderate oven (350)° 10–12 minutes or until golden brown.

Makes about 32 cookies.

BUTTER LEAVES   MÖRDEGSKAKOR

1 cup butter or margarine	*Topping:*
1/2 cup sugar	1 egg white
1 egg yolk	1/3 cup chopped almonds or nuts
1/2 teaspoon almond extract	3 tablespoons sugar
2 1/3 cups sifted all-purpose flour	

Cream butter or margarine; add gradually sugar and cream very well.

Add egg yolk, almond extract and flour. Chill thoroughly.

Work with small amount of dough on lightly floured surface. Roll 1/8-inch thick and cut with floured cutter, shaped like a leaf. Place on buttered cookie sheet. Brush with slightly beaten egg white and sprinkle with chopped almonds mixed with sugar.

Bake in moderate oven (350°) 8–10 minutes or until golden yellow. See color picture facing page 32.

Makes about 70 cookies.

GRANDMOTHER'S
JELLY COOKIES

Buttery and tender, but also very decorative cookies, see color picture facing page 190.

1/2 cup butter or margarine
1/3 cup sugar
1 egg yolk
1/2 teaspoon vanilla extract
12/3 cups sifted all-purpose flour
1/4 teaspoon salt

Topping:
2 tablespoons finely chopped nuts
2 tablespoons sugar
1 egg white

Filling:
2 tablespoons red currant jelly

Cream butter or margarine with sugar until light and fluffy.

Add egg yolk and vanilla and continue to cream.

Sift flour with salt and stir into creamed mixture until well blended; chill thoroughly.

Roll out half of dough on lightly floured surface to 1/8-inch thickness.

Cut out with floured round cookie cutter (about 2 1/2 inches in diameter), place on buttered cookie sheet. Bake in moderate oven (375°) 10–12 minutes; cool.

Roll out remaining dough; cut with scalloped cookie cutter (2 inches in diameter). Cut center from cookies with thimble.

Mix nuts and sugar together on a piece of waxed paper.

Brush cookies with beaten egg white. Lift on tip of spatula and flip into almond-sugar mixture. Press down gently before lifting to cookie sheet.

Bake as described above and cool.

Put dab of red currant jelly in center of each large cookie and place smaller almond coated cookie on top.

Makes about 25 cookies.

JAM SQUARES

Very decorative and wonderful while still slightly warm.

1/2 cup butter or margarine
3 tablespoons sugar
12/3 cups sifted all-purpose flour
1/2 teaspoon baking powder
1/4 teaspoon salt

1 egg yolk
3 tablespoons good jam
** (preferably raspberry jam)**
1 egg white, slightly beaten

Cream butter or margarine; gradually add sugar and cream until well blended.

Sift dry ingredients together.

Stir egg yolk into creamed butter and add flour mixture; mix well and chill thoroughly.

Roll out $^3/_4$ of pastry $^1/_4$-inch thick on waxed paper, making a 7×7-inch square.

Flip pastry on buttered cookie sheet, remove waxed paper and spread surface with jam.

Roll out remaining pastry on lightly floured surface and cut into long, narrow strips. Arrange strips criss cross over jam, brush with beaten egg white.

Bake in moderate oven (375°) for about 15 minutes. Let cake cool 10 minutes and cut into 20 small squares. See color picture facing page 207.

LEMON STARS   CITRONSTJÄRNOR

Good old-fashioned sugar cookies.

$^2/_3$ cup butter or margarine	*Topping:*
$^1/_2$ cup sugar	1 egg white, slightly beaten
1 egg, beaten	2 tablespoons sugar
3 teaspoons grated lemon rind	2 tablespoons chopped nuts
$2^1/_3$–$2^1/_2$ cups sifted all-purpose flour	
$^1/_2$ teaspoon baking powder	

Cream butter or margarine; add sugar gradually and cream until fluffy.

Add egg and lemon rind.

Sift $2^1/_3$ cups of flour and baking powder together and stir into butter mixture. Mix until smooth.

Chill in refrigerator for 1 hour.

Toss on lightly floured surface, using remaining flour if necessary; roll $^1/_8$-inch thick. Cut into stars or other shapes with floured cookie cutter. Brush with beaten egg and sprinkle with sugar. Place on buttered cookie sheets.

Bake in moderate oven (350°) for 8–10 minutes.

Makes about 50 cookies.

FINNISH BREAD

FINSKA BRÖD

One of the most well-known and best liked cookie recipes that has come from Sweden, despite its name.

1 cup sifted all-purpose flour
1/4 teaspoon salt
1/4 cup sugar
1/3 cup ground unblanched
  almonds
1/2 teaspoon vanilla extract
1/2 cup butter

Topping:
1 egg white, slightly beaten
1/4 cup chopped almonds
3 tablespoons sugar

Combine flour, salt, sugar and almonds in bowl.

Add vanilla; cut in butter with 2 knifes or pastry blender, until mixture forms a soft dough. Divide into 4 parts.

Flour hands and roll out dough on floured surface into 4 long strips, the size of your index finger.

Place the 4 strips parallel with each other, and with ruler for a guide, cut through the 4 strips at 1$^{1}/_{2}$-inch intervals.

Brush with egg white and sprinkle with almonds and sugar.

Place on buttered cookie sheet about $^{1}/_{2}$-inch apart.

Bake cookies in moderate oven (350°) 10–12 minutes or until golden yellow. Leave on cookie sheet until cool; remove with sharp knife.

Makes about 50 cookies.

SWEDISH PUNSCH RINGS

PUNSCHRINGAR

1/2 cup butter or margarine
1 cup sifted all-purpose flour
1 tablespoon Swedish Punsch
  or rum

Topping:
1 egg, beaten
8 chopped almonds
2 tablespoons sugar

Cream butter or margarine until white.

Add flour and Swedish Punsch or rum. Mix until well blended.

Roll out on lightly floured surface into strips the size of your index finger and about 4-inch long. Shape into rings. Brush with egg.

Flip egg side down, into almond and sugar mixture. Place on buttered cookie sheet.

Bake in moderate oven (375°) for 8–10 minutes.

Makes about 24 cookies.

RYE COOKIES

1 cup butter
$^1/_2$ cup sugar
1 cup sifted light rye flour
$1^1/_4$ cups sifted all-purpose flour

Cream butter; gradually add sugar and cream until fluffy.
Add rye flour first, then all-purpose flour. Blend well; chill.
Pinch off a small piece of dough at a time, leaving the rest in refrigerator.
Knead dough lightly and roll out dough as thin as possible on well floured surface. Prick surface with fork. Cut rounds with floured cookie cutter about $2^1/_2$ inches in diameter. Cut center from cookies with thimble and prick cookies with a fork. Place on buttered cookie sheets.
Bake in moderate oven (350°) 8–10 minutes or until golden yellow. Leave on cookie sheets to cool.
Makes about 50 cookies.

OLDFASHIONED SPICE COOKIES
BRUNA BRÖD

2 teaspoons whole cardamom seeds
2 cups sifted all-purpose flour
1 cup light brown sugar
1 teaspoon baking powder
1 teaspoon cinnamon
$^1/_4$ teaspoon ground cloves
$^1/_2$ cup chopped, unblanched almonds
1 egg yolk
$^3/_4$ cup butter or margarine

Crush cardamom seeds with a rolling pin or pound in mortar with a pestle. Remove the white hulls.
Place all ingredients in a large bowl, with the butter or margarine on top. Cut butter into the flour mixture with two knives or a pastry blender until it looks like corn meal.
Collect particles between floured hands and knead dough lightly until smooth. Shape into a long roll; chill.
Cut off small pieces and roll into balls.
Place on buttered cookie sheets, flatten slightly with a fork criss-cross wise and sprinkle with sugar.
Bake in moderate oven (350°) 8–10 minutes or until light brown.
Makes about 45 cookies.

CHOCOLATE FAVORITES

1 cup butter or margarine
$3/_4$ cup sugar
1 egg
2 tablespoons cocoa
2 teaspoons vanilla extract
$1^3/_4$ cups sifted all-purpose flour
$1/_4$ teaspoon baking powder

1 egg white, slightly beaten
$1/_4$ cup chopped nuts
3 tablespoons sugar

Cream butter or margarine with sugar. Mix in egg, cocoa and vanilla. Sift flour and baking powder together. Add to creamed mixture. Blend well.

Spread batter on buttered cookie sheets so that you have long strips $1^1/_2$ inches wide and about $1/_4$-inch thick; leave about 3 inches between strips. Brush with egg white and sprinkle with chopped nuts and sugar.

Bake in moderate oven (350°) for about 10–12 minutes. Leave on cookie sheets to cool. After about 2 minutes, cut strips into bars about $1^1/_2$ inches wide. Do not remove from sheet until the cookies are cool and crisp.

Makes about 60 cookies.

CHEWY CHOCOLATE NUT SQUARES

$1/_3$ cup butter or margarine
1 cup brown sugar
1 egg
$1^1/_2$ teaspoons vanilla extract
1 cup sifted all-purpose flour
1 teaspoon baking powder

1 cup semi-sweet chocolate pieces
$2/_3$ cup chopped pecans

Melt butter or margarine; while still hot add brown sugar and stir well. Add egg and vanilla, beat mixture until fluffy.

Sift flour with baking powder, stir into batter. Add chocolate pieces and nuts.

Butter an 8-inch square cake pan, spoon batter evenly into pan.

Bake in moderate oven (350°) 25–30 minutes or until just done. (If overbaked cookies will not be chewy.)

Cool a few minutes before cutting into squares.

Makes 16 squares.

232

CHOCOLATE BROWNIES

CHOKLADSNITT

3 squares unsweetened baking
  chocolate

2/3 cup butter or margarine

1 cup sugar

2 eggs

1/2 teaspoon vanilla extract

2/3 cup sifted all-purpose flour

1/2 cup broken nut meats

Chocolate Frosting:

2 tablespoons cream or top milk

1 egg

1/2 cup sugar

1 1-ounce square unsweetened
  baking chocolate

2 tablespoons butter or margarine

1/2 teaspoon vanilla extract

Melt chocolate over low heat.

Cream butter or margarine, gradually add sugar and beat until fluffy.

Add eggs, one at a time, chocolate, vanilla and flour and mix until blended. Stir in finely broken nuts.

Bake in slow oven (325°) in a buttered 9-inch square cake pan 30–40 minutes, depending upon how moist you like the brownies. For moist cookies 30 minutes is enough, for drier and crispier cookies use longer baking time.

Remove from heat, let cool. Spread with Chocolate Frosting. Cut in 2-inch squares. See color picture facing page 206.

Makes 36 brownies.

Frosting:

Combine frosting ingredients: bring to a boil, stirring constantly. Remove from heat and place in refrigerator until cool.

Beat until of spreading consistency. Spread over cooled brownies.

REFRIGERATOR COOKIES

BRYSSELKÄX

1 cup butter or margarine

2 teaspoons vanilla extract

1/2 cup sugar

2 1/2 cups sifted all-purpose flour

Cream butter or margarine with vanilla and sugar until light and fluffy.

Add flour and blend thoroughly.

Shape dough into rolls, 1 1/2 inches in diameter.

Roll in sugar mixed with cocoa, wrap in waxed paper; chill.

Cut rolls with sharp knife into 1/8-inch thick slices. Place on buttered cookie sheets.

Bake in moderate oven (350°) 6–8 minutes.

Leave on cookie sheet to cool.

Makes about 60 cookies.

This is how Checkerboard Cookies are made
Så här gör man schackrutor

CHECKERBOARD COOKIES SCHACKRUTOR

Make one batch of Refrigerator Cookies, see page 233.

Divide dough into 2 portions. Add 2 tablespoons of cocoa to one portion and work until cocoa is evenly mixed.

Shape each portion into 2 slim rolls; put the four rolls parallel, but alternate in color, together so that a cut slice will form a checkerboard square, see picture above. (The rolls will hold together better, if you brush the joining surface with slightly beaten egg white.)

Wrap rolls in waxed paper; chill.

Cut with sharp knife into $1/4$-inch thick slices. Place on buttered cookie sheets.

Bake in moderate oven (350°) 6–8 minutes.

Makes about 60 cookies.

See color picture facing page 207.

DAINTY NUT BALLS

These cookies usually get finished sooner than any other kind. Try them on your family and find out for yourself.
They are very easy to make too.

$2/3$ cup butter or half butter substitute
1 cup coarsely chopped pecan or walnuts
1 cup plus 1 tablespoon all-purpose flour
3 tablespoons sugar
1 teaspoon vanilla extract

Cream butter in small mixing bowl, and add remaining ingredients. Mix until well blended; chill.

Pinch off small pieces of mixture and roll between floured hands into balls; place on buttered cookie sheets dusted with flour.

Bake in moderate oven (375°) for 8–10 minutes.

Sprinkle cookies, while warm, with confectioners' sugar.

Makes about 40 cookies.

HAZELNUT MACAROONS

NÖTMAKARONER

Inexpensive and good, crunchy cookies.

$3/4$ cup hazelnut or filberts
1 egg, separated
$1/2$ cup sugar

Grind nuts through nut grinder or food chopper.

Mix egg yolk and sugar in small mixing bowl until well blended. Add ground nuts and chill mixture until slightly firm.

Beat egg white until it holds stiff, but not dry peaks. Fold into nut mixture.

Drop batter from teaspoon onto a buttered and floured cookie sheet. Place half a nut on each cookie (optional).

Bake in moderate oven (350°) 10–12 minutes or until lightly browned.

Remove from cookie sheet and sprinkle with confectioners' sugar.

Makes about 25 cookies.

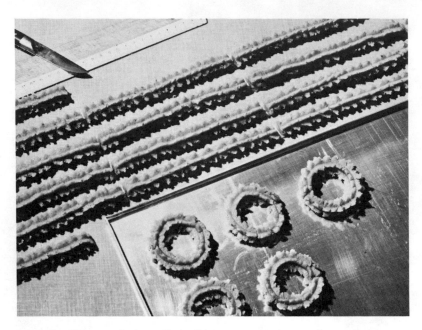

Preparing Cinnamon Spritz or Spritz Rings
Kanelspritskransar

CINNAMON SPRITZ

KANELSPRITS-
KRANSAR

$1/2$ cup butter or margarine

$1/4$ cup confectioners' sugar

5 finely chopped almonds

$1/4$ teaspoon almond extract

$3/4$ teaspoon cinnamon

$1/2$ egg, beaten

$1^1/4$ cups sifted all-purpose flour

Cream butter or margarine, add sugar and cream until fluffy.

Add remaining ingredients and blend thoroughly.

Place dough in cookie press and press into long strips, placing them parallel. Use a ruler to cut off 4-inch long pieces. Shape these into rings. See picture above.

Bake in moderate oven (350°) 12–15 minutes.

Makes about 30 cookies.

236

CINNAMON COOKIES

KANELKAKOR

Flavorful and delicate.

$2/3$ cup butter or margarine

1 cup sugar

1 egg

1 teaspoon vanilla extract

$1^1/_3$ cups sifted all-purpose flour

1 teaspoon baking powder

Topping:

$1/_4$ cup finely chopped nuts

1 tablespoon cinnamon

1 tablespoon sugar

Cream butter or margarine; gradually add sugar and cream thoroughly. Add egg and vanilla. Beat well.

Sift flour and baking powder. Add to creamed mixture. Chill dough.

Mix nuts, cinnamon and sugar.

Mold dough the size of a walnut. Roll each ball in the mixture of chopped nuts, cinnamon, and sugar.

Place balls $2^1/_2$ inches apart on buttered cookie sheet. Bake in moderate oven (350°) 12–15 minutes.

Makes about 60 cookies.

DREAM COOKIES

DRÖMMAR

For these delicate cookies use only butter, because that is what gives them their special flavor.

1 cup butter

$3/_4$ cup sugar

2 teaspoons vanilla extract

1 teaspoon baking powder

$2^1/_2$ cups sifted all-purpose flour

$1/_3$ cup blanched almonds

Melt butter in skillet; continue to heat until it has a golden brown color. Pour slowly into large mixing bowl, so that the thick particles in the butter, which stick to the pan, are not poured off. Cool off a while before placing bowl in refrigerator; allow to stand until butter is firm.

Add sugar and vanilla to firm butter. Beat until very light and fluffy.

Sift baking powder with flour. Add to sugar mixture a little at a time, mixing thoroughly.

Shape dough into small balls. Place on well buttered and floured cookie sheets. Top each cookie with half an almond. See color picture facing p. 206.

Bake in slow oven (325°) for about 25 minutes, or until golden brown. Allow cookies to cool completely before removing from cookie sheets.

Makes about 80 cookies.

Party Cookies
Kalaskakor

PARTY COOKIES KALASKAKOR

These cookies are called "Party Cookies" in Swedish, because they are so attractive looking, see color picture facing p. 207, but also because they are rich and have such a good flavor.

Pastry:	Filling:
$1/2$ cup butter or margarine	**$3/4$ cup blanched almonds**
3 tablespoons sugar	**$1/2$ cup sugar**
1 egg yolk	**1 egg white**
$1^1/2$ cups sifted all-purpose flour	**$1^1/2$ teaspoons water**
	$3/4$ teaspoon almond extract
	5 drops green food coloring

Pastry:

Cream butter or margarine; gradually add sugar and continue to cream until fluffy.

Add egg yolk and flour. Mix thoroughly. Chill pastry for 30 minutes.

Filling:

Grind almonds through a nutgrinder or food chopper and mix with remaining ingredients.

238

Shape pastry into a roll and place on a waxed paper. Roll out pastry to a 10 × 7-inch rectangel.

Spread almond filling over pastry and roll up lengthwise as a jelly roll. Wrap in waxed paper and chill.

Cut roll with sharp knife crosswise into ¼-inch thick slices. Place on well-buttered and floured cookie sheet. See picture, page 238.

Bake in moderate oven (375°) 10–12 minutes.

Makes about 30 cookies.

Do not store these cookies too long, because the almond paste dries out and makes cookies hard instead of chewy.

ORANGE NUT SQUARES   APELSINSNITT

Be prepared to hand out recipes with these cookies, they are most popular.

Bottom Layer:

1/2 cup butter or margarine

1 tablespoon grated orange rind

1/4 cup sugar

1 egg

1¼ cup sifted all-purpose flour

Top Layer:

1½ cups light brown sugar

2 eggs, beaten

2/3 cup chopped nuts

2/3 cup shredded cocoanut

2 tablespoons grated orange rind

2 tablespoons orange juice

2 tablespoons all-purpose flour

1/2 teaspoon baking powder

Bottom Layer:

Cream butter or margarine with orange rind and sugar.

Add egg and flour and mix until well blended.

Pat pastry in bottom of buttered 9-inch square pan.

Bake in moderate oven (350°) for 15 minutes.

Top Layer:

Add brown sugar to beaten eggs, and beat a few minutes on high speed. Stir in nuts, cocoanut, orange rind and orange juice.

Add flour and baking powder and stir until well blended.

Spread mixture over the baked bottom layer.

Return to oven and bake about 20–30 minutes or until a tester inserted in the middle comes out dry and the cake is golden brown.

Dust surface with confectioners' sugar and cut into desired shapes. See color picture facing page 206.

These cookies keep well, if packed in air tight container, either at room temperature or in freezer.

Makes about 20 cookies.

OLD-FASHIONED PRETZELS KRINGLOR

These are rich, old-fashioned cookies, easy to make and good to eat.

3/4 cup butter or margarine
4 tablespoons heavy cream   *Topping:*
2 cups sifted all-purpose flour   1 egg white, slightly beaten
1/4 teaspoons salt   3 tablespoons sugar

Cream butter or margarine until soft, add heavy cream, flour and salt; mix quickly until blended.

Pinch off small pieces of dough, roll out on floured board to 8-inch long, thin strips. Twist ends together and shape into a pretzel.

Brush cookies with egg white and dip in sugar.

Place cookies on buttered cookie sheets. Bake in hot oven (400°) about 8 minutes or until golden yellow.

Makes about 30 pretzels. See color picture facing page 207.

Variation:

Instead of shaping dough into pretzels, roll 1/4-inch thick on lightly floured surface. Cut out round cookies with a cookie cutter (2¹/₄ inches in diameter), which has a hole in the center, and continue as above.

OATMEAL WAFERS HAVREFLARN

Crisp, tasty and easy to make. One of my favorite recipes when I am short of time.

1/2 cup butter or margarine   2 tablespoons sifted all-purpose
3/4 cup sugar   flour
1 teaspoon cinnamon   1 teaspoon baking powder
1 cup oatmeal   1 egg

Melt butter or margarine in saucepan. Remove from heat.

Stir in remaining ingredients and mix until well blended.

Butter cookie sheets very well and dust with flour.

Drop batter from teaspoon onto cookie sheets, 3 inches apart. Bake in moderate oven (375°) about 6–8 minutes or until golden brown. Let stand 1–2 minutes before removing.

Remove wafers quickly from cookie sheet with sharp knife and cool, see picture, next page.

Store in covered box to keep crisp.

Makes about 45 cookies.

Oatmeal Wafers
Havreflarn

Christmas Crullers
Klenäter

CHRISTMAS CRULLERS   KLENÄTER

These cookies are traditional for Christmas and are often served as a dessert with jam in the southern part of Sweden.

4 egg yolks
$1/2$ cup sifted confectioners' sugar
3 tablespoons butter, soft but not melted
1 tablespoon brandy
2 teaspoons grated lemon rind
$1/4$ teaspoon salt
$1^1/4$ cups sifted all-purpose flour

Beat egg yolks for a few minutes. Add sugar and butter. Blend well.

Stir in brandy, lemon rind, salt and as little flour as possible. Work dough quickly on floured surface until smooth. Chill dough thoroughly.

Roll out dough to about $1/8$-inch thick. Cut in strips about 1 inch wide and 3 inches long, preferably with a pastry wheel. Cut a 1-inch slit in center of strips, slip one end through slit, see picture, page 241.

Fry in hot (375°) deep fat until light brown on one side, turn and brown other side. Drain on absorbent paper. Sprinkle with confectioners' sugar. See color picture facing page 190.

Makes about 50 cookies.

ROSETTES   STRUVOR

These old-fashioned delicacies are amazingly easy to make, if you follow the instructions carefully.

2 eggs
1 egg yolk
$3/4$ cup heavy cream
$1/3$ cup sugar
1 cup sifted all-purpose flour
$1/4$ teaspoon salt

Mix eggs, egg yolk and cream together.

Sift sugar, flour and salt together. Sift dry ingredients into egg mixture, a little at a time. Mix thoroughly. Pour into wide shallow dish.

Frying Rosettes in deep fat
Struvor

Place fat in deep fat fryer, or saucepan; place rosette iron in fat. Heat slowly until fat reaches 370°; if you do not have a thermometer, test heat of fat with small piece of white bread, it should get golden yellow within a few moments after dropping in fat.

When fat is at proper temperature, remove rosette iron and allow it to cool and drain on absorbent paper for a few minutes. Then dip quickly into well stirred batter so that batter coats bottom and sides of iron, keeping the top free of batter. Hold iron over batter a few moments so excess batter can run off. Then hold iron over hot fat a few moments before dipping into fat, see picture above. Cook until golden brown. Be careful not to let the iron touch the bottom of the pan or the rosettes will burn.

Remove rosettes from iron with paring knife. Drain on absorbent paper and sprinkle immediately with granulated or confectioners' sugar.

Heat iron again and repeat procedure. Remember to stir batter well each time.

Makes about 40 rosettes.

Homemade Candies

INEXPENSIVE, GOOD CARAMELS   CHOKLADKOLA

1 cup sugar
1 cup dark corn syrup
1/2 cup water
2 tablespoons butter or margarine
4 1-ounce squares unsweetened chocolate
1 teaspoon vanilla extract

Boil together for 6 minutes sugar, corn syrup and water.

Add butter or margarine and boil until candy thermometer reaches 230°, or mixture forms soft ball in cold water.

Drop in chocolate and vanilla and continue boil until thermometer reaches 240°, or mixture forms hard ball in cold water.

Pour into shallow, buttered 8-inch square pan.

Cool, cut into squares, and wrap in waxed paper.

Makes 4 dozen.

SWEDISH TOFFEE   GRÄDDKOLA

2 1/2 cups sugar
1 1/2 cups dark corn syrup
4 tablespoons cocoa
1 cup heavy cream
1 cup light cream
6 tablespoons butter or margarine
1 teaspoon vanilla extract

Combine sugar, syrup, cocoa, creams, and 3 tablespoons butter or margarine in saucepan. Cook over low heat, stirring occasionally, until mixture forms firm ball, which does not flatten, when dropped into very cold water, (250° on your candy thermometer). Stir in remaining butter a little at a time; add vanilla.

Pour into a well buttered 9 × 9-inch cake pan. Cool slightly. Cut in small squares with oiled scissors or sharp knife. Wrap pieces in waxed paper.

Makes 2 pounds toffee.

Swedish Hard Candies being filled into their little paper cups
Knäck fylls i formar eller strutar

SWEDISH HARD CANDIES   KNÄCK

1 cup sugar
1 cup dark corn syrup
$1/4$ cup butter or margarine
1 cup cream
1 cup chopped blanched almonds or mixed nuts

Combine sugar, syrup, butter or margarine and cream in saucepan. Cook over low heat, stirring occasionally, until mixture forms a firm ball, which does not flatten, when dropped in very cold water (250° on your candy thermometer).

Add nuts and pour into small fluted waxed paper candy cups, see picture above, or onto well buttered cookie sheet. (If poured onto cookie sheet, allow to set before cutting into small squares with oiled scissors. Wrap in waxed paper.)

Makes about 60 candies.

COOKING

BAKING

Swedish Index

COOKING

254

44

255

Swedish Index

BAKING